Like Rolling Uphill

Realizing the Honesty of Atheism

by
Dianna Narciso

Llumina Press

ISBN: 1-932560-74-2
Printed in the United States of America by Llumina Press

Contents

For my husband

Chapter One

To Begin With

I remember well the first time I came out to a Christian family member; my body tingled with fear and my face grew hot. I didn't know what she would do or say—I didn't know what I should do or say. I carefully avoided the "A" word, saying simply that I didn't believe in God. Her reaction was mild surprise and a question: "Are you an atheist?" My response was a mumbled, "yes," followed by weak support for Jesus as "okay by me" thrown in as an apologetic afterthought. She was curious and open; though she didn't seem to mind that I didn't believe, she felt I was wrong and recommended a book on the subject. I agreed to read it and let her know exactly what I thought of it. Big mistake.

Maybe the resulting argument wasn't entirely my fault. Perhaps she hadn't actually read the book she recommended, the one that said atheists are immoral, irrational, hopeless and depressed. She may not have known it was merely an angry diatribe against nonbelief and instead rather hoped it would lead me to see things from her perspective. But I reacted as if she, herself, had written the book; I was hurt and insulted and let my thoughts be known. Clue to the clueless: most people don't really want to know what you think; they want you to think like they do.

Humanity is a silly species. It's a good feeling to be able to say that now, because for so long I didn't find anything remotely humorous about it. Early on I thought people were rather stupid, but for the most part well-intentioned. After realizing atheism, I went through a phase when I thought people were hateful, cruel, and ignorant—certain book recommendations didn't help. I noticed, though, that there were others like me in the world who weren't fuming...they were entertained. These people watched John Hagee and Benny Hinn for a good belly laugh when I couldn't stand to listen to them. I wanted to laugh too; it's a lot more fun to let the foibles of a silly species amuse you, than it is to be fearful of them. It took me a long time to understand people well enough to laugh, and even now the humor is tempered by sadness.

Being an atheist in the United States is like being Neo, walking around inside the Matrix watching all the batteries living their lives believing they see reality. Or, it's like being Captain Kirk in "The Return of the Archons" episode of *Star Trek*, puzzling over the behavior of the "followers" of Landru and trying to avoid being absorbed into "the Body." Sometimes I want to shake the whole of humanity and scream, "Wake up!" But it wouldn't work because what they're doing is natural to them; it's a part of what makes them human. The methods used to untangle the web of theism and loosen its grip on each person differ. For some, nothing will work because they are so entwined both with the illusion and the love of it, that no matter what you show them, they will not see it as it is.

Believers have been defending "The Faith" against nonbelievers from the very beginning. As soon as followers of the Christ cult started spreading the "Good News" that the majority of humanity was doomed to eternal torment, there were nay-sayers. The disagreement is nothing new. Believers think they have a truth that others don't have; they call those others all sorts of names like heretic, infidel, and heathen. The heretics and infidels think the believers have been duped into mistaking a lie for truth. But no matter how much debate is engaged in, nothing changes. Well, that's not entirely true...the theology evolves. With each new attack from science and rationalism, Christianity heals its wounds, shifts its paradigm to accommodate, and moves on. Christianity, as do all types of cultural beliefs, adjusts.

It is wildly apparent that nothing anyone can say will make someone who believes in God simply stop believing in God and there is no amount of persuasion a believer can engage in to force a nonbeliever to start believing. The only reason a person will change is because something within him changes; he, for some reason, starts seeing things a different way. It can't be coerced. In fact, the more you try to induce someone to change his beliefs, the more fervently he will cling to them. When a person is devoted to his beliefs, showing him that he is in error won't make him stop believing; logic doesn't work. The believer may adjust his beliefs to accommodate new information, but he will rarely abandon them. A person will only change his mind when he is open to doing so.

I've heard stories of Christian deconversions. Most claim the process was painful and disturbing. Abandoning a cherished belief can be traumatic, but still they did it. A complicated process of doubt and reason led them away from something they were certain was truth into skepticism. These particular people are lucky; they have seen the world from two places, two sides. Sometimes I wish I could force that process on believers so they could see the world from my perspective, even for just a few moments. We might then finally understand each other.

In my experience, few believers (Christians, to be specific) understand atheism at all and the human propensity is, it seems, to demonize and hate that which we don't understand. I have felt the frustration of being misunderstood and denigrated for choosing the atheist label. People try to tell me what I think, what I believe, and who I am, as if they know me—when they have just met me. Believers attempt to explain atheism and atheists to me; they've told me what a depressing, hopeless life I lead, that I am wicked and willful. If I protest that I am not what they say I am, they simply smile that Collective smile and explain that, though I don't realize it because Satan has blinded me to the Truth, I am, in fact, wicked, desperate and hopeless.

If I do manage to clear up a few misconceptions with one member of the Collective, it does no good—along comes another with the same incorrect assumptions. I suffer under the delusion that if I share with believers what I think and why I think it, what I believe and don't believe and why, some might come to a better understanding of atheism and at the very least, not feel threatened by it. While I would like to explain why I don't believe the Christian message, I know I won't convince anyone that my view is correct. People have their good reasons for believing what they do; but very few Christians seem to understand why atheists don't believe the same things. I'd really like to change that but I wonder if it's possible; I wonder if there isn't some code in the Collective that says members must adhere to a dogmatic definition of atheism and atheists. Or perhaps seeing atheism for what it really is would be a threat to the belief.

I can't speak for all atheists—we're all different—I only speak for myself. And I can't speak to or about all Christians. I know that all Christians are not alike, don't believe the same things or hold the same views; atheists are the same way. There, the labels atheist and Christian have something in common. The terms cover various types of people, uniting them under one common definition while allowing for their differences. Atheists are even more varied than Christians because there is no atheist dogma for us to accept. We all share only one thing in common: no god belief.

I don't expect Christians to accept atheists as friends, although there are many who do. I hope that we can at least allow that not everyone believes the things we do and it's important to learn about those who are different, to try to understand them as best we can so that we can live together peacefully.

What is an atheist?

Everybody seems to think he knows what atheism is and what atheists believe but there is the first clue that something is amiss. The term atheist doesn't tell you anything about what a person believes...only about one thing that he doesn't.

Atheism, in its basic sense, is lack of belief in deity. When someone says he is atheist, that's the only thing you can be sure of: he does not believe in deity—he has no such belief. Some people make a distinction between strong and weak atheism. A strong atheist would assert that gods do not exist or even that they can't possibly exist; a weak atheist only claims he has no belief in any god. The difference is fuzzy, but it is also profound. Strong atheism is a position with respect to god's existence—deity does not exist or I don't believe (or think) it does. Weak atheism is the barest definition of the term and is a description of a person's nonbelief: I don't *believe in* gods.

Many atheists waver between strong and weak atheism. We must, for instance, take the strong position (that gods do not exist) when arguing the matter. It would be pointless to enter a debate on the existence of God with the attitude that God may exist but we simply don't believe it. We can't always live with the certainty we desire in a debate, however. Sometimes in normal conversation or thought, I am a strong atheist, feeling that the idea of deity is nonsensical or impossible. At other times I'm a weak atheist, imagining that deity is possible but acknowledging that I simply do not believe in any.

The theist rebuttal to the strong atheist position is typically to claim that there are, in actuality, no atheists. Imagine my surprise upon hearing that! In order to know that gods do not exist, they say, you would have to know everything...and you can't know everything so the most you can be is agnostic. This is not acceptable reasoning. Do Christians accept the existence of every possible entity because they can't be sure that such an entity does not exist? Can we never make a claim that something doesn't exist?

A favorite example among many atheists is the Invisible Pink Unicorn. Do you believe in the Invisible Pink Unicorn? Does she exist? Is it at all possible for her to exist? You don't know everything, so you can't say she doesn't exist. How about fire-breathing dragons? Are you an agnostic with regard to fire-breathing dragons? You must be; you must claim that you do not know whether they exist or not. This leaves a person in a constant state of "maybe" with regard to all possible entities. Atheists might claim that theists, not having proof of the existence of deity and having to rely on faith, should honestly proclaim agnosticism as well. Because certainty of the existence of gods is impossible, by theistic reasoning, we must all be agnostics.

When deciding the question of the existence of gods, the strong atheist weighs the evidence and decides against the proposition: gods are not evident, therefore, the probability of their existence is minute so, for all intents and purposes, gods do not exist. I know that gods don't exist in the same manner that I know fairies, gnomes and unicorns don't exist. I have no evidence for their existence. There is no need to form a belief about them. I, in the same manner, have no need to build a belief around a deity for whom I have no evidence.

Theists claim there is adequate evidence for a creator; I have studied all that has been presented to me, but have found it lacking. Therefore, it is quite reasonable for me to claim strong atheism: gods do not exist—at least until such time as evidence might prove otherwise. With regard to the Christian Bible god, not only do I find no evidence of its existence, but I find it logically inconsistent and contradictory. I am, therefore, more certain of the nonexistence of that particular god than of any other.

An atheist, though, is not someone who steadfastly denies the existence of deity as if it is proven fact; atheists know they can't prove god's nonexistence, but, we may reasonably deny the existence of deity because there is no evidence that such exists. There is no reason to be continually on the lookout for deity any more than one must continually look out for elves. There is even less must continually look out for elves. There is even less reason to create a belief about deity in light of the lack of evidence.

Agnostic is supposed to mean "without knowledge." An agnostic might claim that we can't know if gods exist. They would be more likely to say they don't know if a god exists or not, as to say, as many atheists do, that no gods are evident therefore they do not exist. Agnostics generally have no *belief* in deity, so to me they are atheists; they don't believe in gods. I suppose it can be said that the agnostic, while claiming no knowledge of deity, is free to believe in deity and still remain agnostic. He would say, "I don't know if it exists for certain, but I believe in it." I've never met such agnostics, but I'm sure they're out there.

On *The Secular Web* at *www.infidels.org* I have had the pleasure of reading debates on the atheist versus agnostic positions, their meanings, their uses as labels, and their relationship. The best I can say about them is that you can never assume to know what a person means when applying the labels atheist or agnostic to himself. It is always best to find out from the individual just what form his nonbelief takes.

If you want to play the semantics game, you could say that everyone is an atheist. The deists believe that there was a god that started everything, set the universe in motion, then left or sat back to watch. It isn't a personal god and certainly isn't the one in the Bible. That makes deists without belief in any number of gods and therefore atheist with respect to them.

Pantheists too are atheist. They believe that the universe itself is god. They certainly are atheist with respect to all the myriad gods of history, especially the traditional Western god. Those who practice nature religions don't believe in gods, but rather spirits and other supernatural entities, therefore, they are atheist.

Christians and Jews, too, are atheist with respect to all other gods but their own. In other cultures, it is Christians who are atheists. Stephen Roberts, a widely-quoted atheist on the Internet, said,

I contend that we are both atheists. I just believe in one fewer god than you do. When you understand why you dismiss all the other possible gods, you will understand why I dismiss yours.

(From Stephen F. Roberts' Freelinks at
http://wildlink.com/freelink /index.sht)

It is important to understand the distinct difference between atheists and Christians. Atheists don't believe in any gods while Christians don't believe in all gods save one. Very simply, when you understand why you don't believe in Zeus or Vishnu, you will understand why I don't believe in your god.

I don't consider everyone atheist simply because there are some gods in which they don't believe. To me, an atheist is someone who doesn't believe that any gods exist or has no god belief. When I meet someone, I let them define themselves. I wish that others would grant me the same ability: to describe myself and my label as I use it. Instead, I am *told* what atheism is by someone who is not one himself and what they tell me I am is rarely the truth about me.

Where did this misunderstanding of atheism originate? It isn't all the fault of theists, though they define atheism on their own terms by claiming they know that God is real and atheists deny his obvious existence. Atheists too, have claimed different meanings for the word.

As quoted in *Bertrand Russell on God and Religion* (Prometheus, 1986), in an article published in *Look* magazine in 1953, Russell said that:

> An atheist, like a Christian, holds that we *can* know whether or not there is a God. The Christian holds that we can know there is a God; the atheist, that we can know there is not. The agnostic suspends judgment, saying that there are not sufficient grounds either for affirmation or for denial. At the same time, an agnostic may hold that the existence of God, though not impossible, is very improbable; he may even hold it so improbable that it is not worth considering in practice. In that case, he is not far removed from atheism.

Did you get that? Russell said that atheists think they can know there is not a god. Many atheists would not accept this definition. I do think that the lack of evidence for deity is sufficient to accept its non-existence; but I also believe that it can not be known with absolute certainty. It is so close to certain, however, that I reasonably claim strong atheism. I am not so sure that all agnostics suspend judgment. I have little doubt that agnostics call themselves agnostic for all manner of reasons.

Agnosticism was first coined as a label by Thomas Huxley. George Smith, in *Atheism: The Case Against God* (Prometheus, 1989), writes:

> It seems that Huxley originally meant this term as some-what of a joke. He selected the early religious sect known as "Gnostics" as a prime example of men who claim knowledge of the supernatural without justification; and he distinguished himself as an "a-gnostic" by stipulating that the supernatural, even if it exists, lies beyond the scope of human knowledge. We cannot say if it does or does not exist, so we must suspend judgment.

Does the agnostic really suspend judgment? He doesn't act as if the supernatural and gods might exist, does he? I haven't met one yet who does. Sometimes the way we live our daily lives says one thing about us and our philosophical labeling says another. Philosophically a person could be an agnostic; when pressed on the matter he may claim that the answer to the god question is inherently unknowable. But he lives his life as if no god exists just as the atheist does. I can't say I am any different from an agnostic in that respect; if there is a supernatural entity out there, we don't know anything about it. But I don't suspend judgment entirely. If it's there but is unknowable, there is no difference between its existence and its nonexistence therefore it may just as well not exist as exist; so as far as I'm concerned, it doesn't. But most importantly, I don't *believe* it does.

Why do the agnostics get better treatment from the Christian community? If you define agnosticism as mere doubt, the agnostic seems to say, "I don't know, you might have something there but I'll withhold judgment on it." If you define atheism as outright refutation, the atheist seems to say, "There is no god; I don't believe it." With the agnostic, then, the Christian might sense an honest questioning and with the atheist, an abrupt denial. Because the Christian claims that in order to experience God you must be open to the possibility of his existence, he would naturally be antagonistic toward someone he thinks flatly denies that possibility. I don't feel these are adequate portrayals of agnosticism and atheism. They are both a lack of belief in deity for perhaps shades of different reasons. Many, if not most, atheists do not deny the possibility of deity but they claim the label atheist because they feel it best describes their position with respect to deity—they don't believe in it.

How are people atheists?

There are a few ways people find themselves to be atheist. You could be taught to accept atheism uncritically, you could fail to or refuse to consider the question of deity, or you could arrive at the conclusion rationally. The best pathway to atheism, in my opinion, is through rationalism. Any other approach is not well-grounded.

Indoctrination and atheist parenting

To be atheist only because you were taught to be without examining the question of god's existence critically would be a sad state of being. Claiming that gods do not exist, that you don't believe in any, only because someone you consider an authority has told you so is not acceptable, in the same way that believing in a god because someone else has told you it exists is not acceptable. Atheist parents must be careful not to "indoctrinate" their children with atheism. But what is indoctrination?

There are no gods; that is apparent to me as I have not seen, heard from nor experienced any. I have no problem discussing the prospect of gods with my children. It can be fun to imagine the possibilities of what life is all about, where it came from, what the universe is, etc. But, after thoroughly studying Christianity, through the Bible and history, I am fairly certain the Christian god doesn't exist. I can't tell my children that perhaps it does, any more than I can tell my children that perhaps fire-breathing dragons or monsters exist. If I should tell my child that, yes, it's *possible* that the Christian god exists and if you don't believe in him and worship him properly a terrible punishment awaits you after death, how then am I to deny that it is *possible* that an invisible monster is indeed under his bed at night and may take him away and torture him? How can I deny one and not the other when, in my view, the evidence for both is equal—they are both characters from stories in books? Let me say that again for proper effect. The evidence for monsters under the bed and for the existence of the Christian god is equal. For the same reasons I reject monsters, I reject the existence of Jehovah.

I have heard of parents who spray water around the bedroom pretending to ward off ogres or spend several minutes exposing all possible hiding places proving them free of imaginary creatures. I don't do these things because I will not tell my child that his fears are reasonable when they are not. I tell my children that it is understandable to be afraid, but that monsters are fictional characters in books. Fictional characters aren't real. There's no need to spray the room with monster repellent; there's no need to check the corners. Monsters could not possibly be in the room because they do not exist.

Telling my child that monsters do not exist is not indoctrinating him against monsters. Telling him that fairies, gnomes and elves do not exist is not indoctrination. Telling him that dinosaurs, no matter how real they are made to look in movies, are extinct and no longer roam the Earth is not indoctrination. Teaching my children that fantastic things they read about in books and see in movies are fiction, is not indoctrination. And telling my child that gods do not exist is also not indoctrination.

Indoctrination would mean instilling in my child a doctrine of belief. It is telling my child: this is what you must believe; you must accept this and not that. How then, does an atheist parent keep from indoctrinating his children? Simply by not ever telling him what he *must* believe. Children should be taught to think rationally and be skeptical of all claims, and they should be allowed to use their critical thinking skills in determining what is true and what is not.

The question of gods, when it comes up—and it will—can be discussed and examined as is any other claim. Your child must be allowed to discover possibilities and explore beliefs but certainly he must always be expected to exercise critical thinking at his age level. My children, each in turn, expressed a belief in a god of some sort at different times in their youth. I never discouraged them, never told them they were wrong, or silly. I accepted their belief. I also never lied. When they asked me—and they always did—if I believed, I said no. When they asked me why, I was as honest as I could be. That is not indoctrination; it's honest parenting.

However, it must be noted that we live in a world where god belief is the norm. It would be inadequate for me to simply tell my children that as far as I can tell there are no gods, without also explaining to them that most people believe there are. As an atheist parent, I consider it part of my job to teach my children about all the world's religions from Christianity, Judaism and Islam, to ancient paganism, Wicca and Native American spirituality. I have read African and Asian creation myths to my children; we explored Bible stories; we compared and discussed religions. I never told my children they must believe one of them over another and I certainly never told my children they must not believe in any of them.

I hear a little Christian voice in the back of my head, saying, "But you presented the Christian God as myth to your children; you controlled their ability to accept him as real." That's right. I read the Christian story of creation alongside other cultural stories of creation and my children never batted an eyelid. Not once did they say, "Boy, the Christian story sounds so true, so possible, and so different than those other stories!" Not once—because the Christian story reads the same as the other myths. There is no reason other than cultural programming and parental indoctrination to believe that the Christian myth is anything more than all the other myths of history. In other words, and this is very important, I didn't have to tell my children the Christian story was a myth; they were able to discern that for themselves.

Atheism without much thought

Traveling through life never considering the idea of deity is acceptable. For some of us, the concept is never brought to the fore, the question never arises. However, once you consider the proposal seriously you have a decision to make: will you accept that gods do not exist because someone tells you they do not? Will you accept that one or another god does exist because someone tells you it does? Will you read one of the holy books and believe in one of the deities told of in it because the author of the book says it exists? Or will you weigh the evidence for yourself and use your reason to determine your stance?

Many people might say that the question of gods is nonsensical and a stance is not necessary. This is certainly acceptable and is, actually, grounded in reason. Such a person, in declaring the term god meaningless, has used his knowledge of the world to make that determination. As long as the person who finds it unnecessary to take a position is not simply deferring the question because he is uncomfortable with it or finds it confusing, he isn't open to attack by theists bent on absorbing him into the Collective. Claiming that a stance is meaningless because god is meaningless is different from ignoring the idea altogether.

There are all sorts of atheists around who have never really examined the question of god's existence. They are everywhere; in all economic and educational levels, in all ethnic and age groups. There are atheists teaching your children, running your government, flipping your burgers, guiding corporations. There are atheists in the churches, the synagogues and mosques. But, they don't all know that they're atheist because they haven't actually considered the matter of the existence of gods.

It is part of human nature that we go along with our society and community or that we continue to do what we were taught to do as children. We do what is comfortable. If going to church is comfortable, or gives us some reward such as a sense of community or business contacts or a feeling of peace and goodness, we continue to go. If not, we quit going, but we may still call ourselves Christian because everyone else we know says they are and we are social animals who crave a feeling of belonging to a group.

From what I can tell through observation and experience, much of the church affair is akin to a weekly self-help workshop as much as it is a gathering to praise and worship a deity. In that respect, I can see the appeal. But, even those people who might secretly suspect they don't agree with the god part of the religious matter seem to be repelled by the idea of atheism.

Taking on the label

The word atheist really bothers people—especially Christians. It is the complete opposite of what believers claim to be, a denial of what they believe, an affront to their belief. I can understand that. If you believe in something and feel that everyone else ought to also, someone blatantly saying you're wrong could be a problem. Even people who don't believe in gods will back away from the label of atheist because of the reaction other atheists have received or because they have fallen for the negative definitions proffered by theists.

"Atheists are rude," one Humanist told me, after confessing he was one himself but wouldn't use the label. I have no doubt that there are rude atheists. There are rude people of every sort. It may be that this man had only met rude atheists because it takes some nerve to go about in this country actually admitting you are atheist. It might be good for atheism if all atheists were kind and considerate...it might be good for Christianity if all Christians were kind and considerate, too; but, that's not the way people work. I'll try not to judge all Christians by the worst I've seen, if others try not to judge all atheists the same way.

There are two kinds of people who are likely to make the bold claim that they are in fact, atheists: those who have thought carefully about their lack of belief and have chosen the label as the best description of that nonbelief, and those who want to piss people off. The teenager who rebels against his family and his religion and spends a few years pretending to disbelieve in his god's existence is not an atheist.

There are Christians who claim they were former atheists. Few of them, upon careful questioning, turn out to have truly been. Atheists do not believe that gods exist. Anyone who believes a god exists but denies that god's authority over his life is not an atheist—he is a rebellious believer. Someone who believes there must be a creator, a supreme being of some kind, but doesn't call that being the Christian God and doesn't believe that Jesus is the son of a god, is not an atheist except in that semantics game we played earlier.

Letters From a Skeptic (SP Publications, 1994) by Gregory A. Boyd was presented to me as a book in which a son converts his atheist father to Christianity through a series of letters between them. Was Mr. Boyd Sr. an atheist? In his preface, Mr. Boyd claims: "Exceptionally intelligent, intensely skeptical, very strong-willed, and seventy years old—could a more *unlikely* candidate for conversion be found than my father?" Yes, a more unlikely candidate could certainly have been found. From the start of their letters, his father admits he believes in a supreme being. His father wasn't an atheist; he was simply a non-Christian theist. Once a person is willing to accept the supernatural, converting him to one's particular brand of supernaturalism isn't such a great feat. It was an achievement; I don't want to discount Mr. Boyd's proselytizing skills. His father was indeed skeptical of Christianity. But, Mr. Boyd did misrepresent his father as the "most unlikely candidate for conversion" to be had! I don't recommend anyone approach an atheist with that book in mind. You must first persuade the atheist that there is a god before you can even begin to convince him he had a son.

Is "god" meaningless?

Some atheists and agnostics will answer the question, "Do you believe in God?" with the statement, "Define god." What is god? God is different things to different people.

I watched a talk show once on the topic of god. One of the audience members stood to tell the host that she didn't believe in god. The host countered with, "Do you believe in love?" The woman answered, "Yes." "Then you believe in god," said the host. How odd. What is it to *believe in* love? The host never bothered to find out in what manner her audience member believed in love, what she meant by believing in it, or what she meant by love. She simply enlarged her circle enough so that the audience member fit in. Why? Because if everyone believes, it's okay for her to believe too!

What does it mean to say god is love? Love is an emotion—a feeling of empathy, adoration, caring, and compassion. It moves us to behave in various ways, not all attractive. Christians like to say that their god *is* love but that is meaningless. In order for their god to be love itself, love must first be considered not an emotion, but an existing force...an entity. Then god becomes some sort of energy-in-motion for good only. Not only does this alter the definition of the emotion love, but it reduces the concept of god to an impersonal force. Yet, the Christian god is said to be a personal god, not an impersonal force; and I've never heard of anyone praying to love.

I must assume they mean that God is all-loving. How one can accept the concept of Hell and an all-loving deity seems an exercise in mental gymnastics; but, that's beside the point. Yes, some people believe that god is, in fact, love itself. If you believe in love you believe in god. That is nonsensical. What is it to believe in love? How does one believe in it? What do you believe about it? How can you pray to love? How does a person worship it?

Some say god is energy. They tend to believe this energy is purposeful and can be used for good, or can be communed with. Some people say the universe is god which reduces the concept to complete nothingness by enlarging it to encompass everything. Why not just talk about the universe? Why bother renaming it, making it more than it is? Why do we have this need to anthropomorphize everything?

Gods are supernatural beings—superior to humans. The Christian god is supposed to be supreme in the universe, a being that supposedly *created* the universe. The term "god" is not meaningless to me, but the being it represents is unknowable and undefined. If there is a being or entity that created the universe and/or the world, we don't know anything about it—neither you nor I—none of us do.

❃❃❃

A brief note on the capitalization of the word god: Throughout history, man has worshiped many gods with many names. God is a common noun, and therefore should not be capitalized in normal usage. The Christian god has different names, probably because it's a combination of several deities. He is called Jehovah and Yahweh; but, because they think he is the only one, Christians most often call him, simply, God. I try to refrain from capitalizing the term unless I am referring specifically to the Christian god, called God. God as a common noun, idea, or concept, remains in lower case.

Chapter Two

My Life

> My father says that almost the whole world is asleep…everybody
> you know, everybody you see, everybody you talk to. He says that
> only a few people are awake and they live in a state of constant,
> total amazement.
> —Patricia Graynamore in the film *Joe Versus the Volcano*
> (Amblin Entertainment/Warner Brothers, 1990)

I am an atheist. I don't believe that gods exist. I also don't believe there is a supernatural realm. I didn't realize I was an atheist until I was in my mid-thirties. Up until that time I thought I was pretty much like everyone else I knew. I believed in god; I talked about god. But there was always the knowledge, deep down, that I was different. One day, that knowledge came to the fore.

It started with a little click in my brain that told me I was tired of being something I was not. All my life I've claimed to be a deep and introspective person, probably because it sounded so wonderful. But while I was thoughtful, as in always daydreaming, I was rarely thoughtful, as in *thinking*. One day, with a little click in my head, I started thinking…and discovered myself.

We humans like to describe ourselves as thinking beings—that's what separates us from the animals, we claim. I have come to accept that most humans spend very little time really thinking; conscious, purposeful thinking isn't something most of us are accustomed to doing. What we do, more often, is go along with the crowd, believing what we're told; we get through life more than truly living it.

Several years ago, I was sitting on a bench at my children's pre-school having a conversation with the mother of my oldest son's classmate. She was (and is) a friendly, outgoing woman with whom I enjoyed conversation. While usually in a fairly good mood, that morning she said she was depressed. I can't remember exactly what her reasons were, but I do recall her saying that she tried and tried to understand God's will for her life but couldn't; she felt lost and confused.

When she said that, I started in with my usual manner of responding to godly talk among acquaintances. First, I reworked *their* version of god into *my* version of god, which at that time was the "god is love" or "god is the energy back of all creation" idea. After translating god, I'd come up with my response such as "love guides us gently" or "we must use the energy in a positive way and let all negativity fall by the wayside in order to feel fulfilled." Then I'd have to rephrase that response into terms that my acquaintance would understand before actually putting the words in my mouth. For instance, I would say, "God is speaking to you through your heart and you need to put away all your anxieties to hear him." I believe I did that when my friend expressed her frustration with learning God's will on that morning so many years ago; but distinctly I remember that after I responded, I stopped listening to her.

Something had happened in my mind and in my emotional self. Something clicked. I can still recall the feeling I had that my face had frozen, that my eyes had clouded. I wasn't looking at my friend anymore. I was somewhere else. I was thinking, as if realizing it for the first time, "I don't believe in god the way she does."

I found that I didn't want to interpret anymore. I was tired of trying to fit my ideas about deity into the typical Biblical Christian idea of deity. Not only did I feel I couldn't filter my beliefs through the sieve of traditional Christianity anymore, I felt I wasn't completely sure of what I believed at all. I drove home from the preschool that day asking myself if I really believed that there was an energy that was love. Did I really believe that there was a particular force that directs the universe? In one of the first completely honest moments of my life, I accepted that I did not believe those things.

For a few days after that, I examined the rest of my beliefs. At that time I subscribed, casually, to what was called Science of Mind originated by Ernest Holmes, who wrote the book with that title. In the Science of Mind that I knew, there was a purposeful energy that could be used in our lives. That energy was love. If you filled your mind with thoughts of love, prosperity, peace and joy, those things would come into your life. If you filled your mind with negativity, hate, envy and greed, only bad things would come to you.

I believed that reincarnation was probable and that creatures evolved progressively with each life to a degree dependant on what was learned in that lifetime. You could not, therefore, be reborn as an animal because animals are not as consciously aware—as evolved in the spiritual sense—as humans. We begin our human period as rather dumb and progress toward total awareness of god. Of course, in that belief, humans are the top of the line and whatever else comes beyond that is supernatural.

I believed there were levels of awareness and that people who believed in the traditional religions such as Biblical Christianity were simply not as evolved as those of us who'd reached a higher level of awareness. Those who were below you on this spiritual grading scale were not to be looked down on though, because we were "all on the same path." However, I never believed in the idea that all paths lead to god, but just travel different routes; I always believed that Christianity and other salvation religions were not the correct path, but that they were the best that *that level* of spirituality could do in that particular lifetime.

I believed that the Earth was created as a place for our spirits to be born and reborn to learn and to play. I believed that "what you think upon grows." And I believed that there was a benevolent nature to the universe.

I no longer believe any of those things. From that moment of realization that I didn't believe anything I thought I did, I found myself on a journey of learning and understanding that, while some spots were difficult and upsetting, was very much like rolling uphill toward self-enlightenment. I couldn't stop the progress, I couldn't stop the momentum, and I certainly couldn't go back to where I'd been. I once thought of the journey as much like peeling away the layers of an onion until my spirit was free to rise out of the empty center...and the tears along the way were the result of the fumes of the useless, bothersome beliefs that had hindered my life up until each significant layer had been shed. Once I started thinking about it like that, the tears weren't so important anymore.

My parents were without religion, but spiritual. They were ships afloat on a sea of hope and imagination—anything could be true if you believed it. In my house, growing up, religion in the traditional sense was a nonissue. Jesus was presumed to have been an extraordinary man, a great teacher. We were all the children of god, all had the capability of being as enlightened as Jesus. Jesus told us that the kingdom of god was within, which clearly meant within each of us. We *are* god, each one of us, like pieces of a pie. God equaled Mind. Because of this, if we could only channel the power of Mind through ourselves, anything was possible (as in: with god, all things are possible).

I remember once my father saying that one day humans would be able to fly...like birds! Because we had it in our minds to fly, built craft to make flying possible, one day, through the power of Mind, we would fly as birds. It seems ridiculous to me now, but back then, I could believe it.

My mother's family was Southern Baptist and her experiences with Christianity in childhood were less than ideal which no doubt helped her to release it and accept New Age philosophies. She didn't abhor traditional religion, however, and for a time when I was about eight years old, she took me to the local Episcopalian church. I was also allowed to visit the churches of my friends.

When I look back on my life, my most honest moments were shrouded in shame. When I stood up and spoke out, I was shamed. When I behaved in the way I honestly wanted to, I was shamed. Is honesty so shameful? Perhaps. Honesty—total, conscious honesty—can get you into trouble. People don't really want you to be honest. They want you to go along with them, with their crowd. You *must* have a crowd. It's best if you are in the *right* crowd, but if you're in another crowd, one that's just a little bit different, that's okay. Even if you're in a crowd that's very different...it's still pretty much okay. Your crowd might be looked down upon by another crowd and vice versa...but at least you are in a crowd. You have to be in some crowd. If you're not, you're *the fringe*. The fringe is dangerous. The fringe thinks, asks, acts. The fringe is honest.

I wasn't in the fringe. I hadn't yet begun to think for myself. I knew I was different, but not so different as to be incompatible with the majority. I felt I was part of a generation at least. We all moved together through elementary, junior high and high school, the same familiar faces year after year. I hovered on the outskirts of various cliques pretending to fit in; I created relationships out of acquaintances. Looking back, I can see that my problem was not that I was odd so much as that I didn't know who I was. No one had taught me that all-important life skill: know thyself.

At some point as a pre-teen, my parents got involved in the religion I mentioned earlier called Science of Mind. Just like any other religion, Science of Mind had some good and some bad in it. What I got out of Science of Mind is simply that the mind controls the being. If you fill your mind with hateful, sad, miserable, bad thoughts, hateful, sad, miserable, bad things will come into your life. What you think on grows. It worked for me as a pre-teen and teenager, when I used it. It helped me to find some happiness, some success, some friendship, but I couldn't use it consistently because I was human and couldn't live in a constant state of positive thought. Maybe it wasn't that I was human so much as that I wasn't stupid. I mean, to a point I can agree with the theory that when you hold onto happy thoughts you will be a happier person but no amount of positive thinking is going to save you if a drunk driver careens your way. Positive thinking on your part can not and does not alter events in your favor—it is not a shield.

By about age twelve, I began to succumb to what I can only describe as extreme PMS. My hormones were in charge, not me. I vacillated between dark, bleak depression, mild weepiness, melancholy, and uncontrollable joy. No, I wasn't manic-depressive; I was going through puberty. I had little control of my emotions, my mind or my body—I was losing it. I managed to muddle through, as most teenagers do but I never turned toward religion and Jesus, as many did.

My mother eventually left the Science of Mind Church, which is nowadays called the Church of Religious Science, over an ideological conflict. Apparently, the leaders of her study group were adamant that any negative thought, no matter how fleeting, would bring a bad result into your life and that you must purge your mind of all negativity. My mother believed that positive thoughts overcame negative thoughts, so you could undo any negativity before it manifested itself in your life. This wasn't party-line, I guess. My mother couldn't accept that positive thinking would become a strict dogma one must adhere to; she also had a degree in psychology and probably knew the limits of the human animal's mind much better than the old ladies in her study group.

In my early teen years, my mother began attending a local Unity church. It was at Unity that I learned the idea of god as the pie and people as individual slices. That is where I was given a copy of a book called *The Big Me and the Little Me*. It was a Cinderella story in which

Cinderella learns that the Big Me is the giving, loving part of herself and the Little Me is the part that people use when they are selfish and stingy...like her stepsisters. The Big Me got the prince and the castle. Believe it or not, that book greatly impacted me and taught me to be more positive. I was still an emotional wreck until puberty was under control but I began to have moments of positive joy and enthusiasm that only grew and grew.

In my early years, belief was not an issue. As an adult, Christianity and faith surrounded me, suffocated me, oppressed me; it was every-where I looked. I heard about it from everyone I met. I read about it every time I opened the newspaper. But as a youth, it was rarely men-tioned. It hardly existed.

I lived on a busy through street, with a huge neighborhood behind me. I played with a group of kids mostly of my older brother's age. One family was Southern Baptist and went to the First Baptist Church in town. I went with them once to see their youngest daughter baptized. I remember she told me that each person had crowns in Heaven—one crown for every good deed. I don't remember believing anything she said but I don't remember not believing it either. Her vision of god, it seemed, was a man in a white robe with a white beard. He sat in a throne in Heaven...a king.

I do remember one discussion in particular about death. We all ar-gued about whether or not a person could come back from the dead and tell about it. There were stories, just as there are now, of near-death ex-periences. I and my brother and perhaps some others were of the mind that if you came back to life, you weren't dead to begin with. The oth-ers argued that if your heart stops beating for a certain length of time, you're dead. Then, if you're revived, you "came back from the dead."

I don't remember how or if the argument was resolved but it did nothing to interfere with the friendships enjoyed by the entire group. We could disagree without problem and the fact that only those South-ern Baptists went to church didn't seem to matter. It was with at least one of those Southern Baptists that we all sat around while one of us read from *The Happy Hooker*. Childhood is different. Childhood is cleaner, more honest, less influenced by the fears that enshroud adult-hood.

I never really broached the subject of god, religion, or Christianity seriously as a child. Later, in high school, I had a few boyfriends whose parents were Christian, but they were open to honest and curious dialogue. One of my more steady boyfriends and I used to get drunk and ponder the big questions of life, the universe and existence. What was there before there was anything? What is *nothing*? Isn't *nothing* something? That's not easy to think on when you're drunk—it's hard enough to think on when you're sober.

One of my favorite acquaintances in high school was Sally (not her real name, of course). Sally was the friendliest girl I have ever known. She always had a smile on her face and never said a bad word to or about anyone; the girl was a saint. But alas, she succumbed. She and I attended a play performed by the youth group of a church in town. The plot was pretty silly, looking back on it, but it wasn't badly acted. It took place on an airplane where there was some discussion about Christ and God and all that. Someone got saved and then the plane crashed. It wasn't enough to show the saved being swept up into the arms of God with a lovely blue light embracing them, they had to go on with the damned being burned by fire for all eternity (thank goodness the play didn't last that long) with a red light blazing down on them.

When the damned were getting their just deserts, Sally's hand slipped into mine and squeezed it tight. I was embarrassed for her; I was shamed for her, that she allowed such maudlin nonsense to stir her. It was pure fiction, in my opinion. Then the worst came. The lights went up and the sheep were called to the altar to be saved. It was all so contrived! First they scared you with the disease and then voila, here's the cure! But Sally got up and got her salvation. She was never quite the same again. While she was still the sweetest girl I knew, there was just the tiniest hint of fear and elitism in her attitude after that. She had found the Truth and she really wished that everyone else would too.

The big church in town was Park Avenue Baptist. Everyone who was anyone, and not Catholic, went to Park Avenue Baptist. They had what they called Joy Explosions on Wednesday nights for the teenagers. I think they were a combination of parties and prayer meetings, on a teenage level. Sally went to them often. She became nervous; she was always concerned with God's will and what God wanted. One day, I came upon her crying in the band room. She'd just come from P.E. where God had told her to announce to all the kids waiting for the bell to ring that the Joy Explosion was that night and they were all welcome to attend. But she didn't do it. She was too afraid to speak up and God would punish her for that, she was sure.

My Science of Mind and Unity teaching came into play and I told her that god would not punish her for being human or for being afraid. God urges us to do right but god is gentle and fair and loving. God forgives. I think I made her feel better...but honestly, I don't remember.

I was lucky enough to belong to a club in school: *Alpha Chi Rho*. I tried to fit in there as best as I could. It turned out to be a Christian club, something I didn't know when I applied for membership (not that it would have made any difference to me). We were supposed to go together to a different local church each month. One of the members was the daughter of a minister and one month we visited her church;I think it was Methodist. At the service we attended, her father the minister told us quite frankly that it wasn't enough for us to be saved and Christian to get into Heaven; if we didn't also go out and claim at least one soul for Christ ourselves, we got Hell! I recall being appalled at such a horrific idea and looking down the row at the other girls as if to say, "Did I hear that right?" But nobody else seemed to notice or care.

These brushes with fundamentalism were rare. For the most part, religion meant nothing to me. I did, however, call myself a Christian. Everyone I knew was Christian and they seemed little different from me, if at all. I included myself in that religious bracket without really thinking about what it meant.

That is how my religious life progressed from then until a few years ago. Whenever god was mentioned, I translated. I took the way they meant god and changed it into what I meant by god. God wasn't a *being*. God *was* being. God wasn't a king, a ruler, a despot who controls, orders and punishes. God was love. God was energy. God was existence itself. I spoke about god to people from my beliefs but always careful to phrase my words so that they would understand them from within their beliefs. At first it was easy. I could comprehend little difference between god as a being and god as *Being*. But as I grew and matured, as my life changed, so did my ability to and my willingness to translate from their beliefs into mine and back again.

Then that something clicked and I started rolling uphill, shedding those layers of belief until I reached the core of total, pure honesty that had only occasionally bubbled to the surface in my life up to then. The journey was not without its bumps and pains, but overall, it was exhilarating and educational beyond belief—no pun intended, of course.

The first thing I did, after realizing that I didn't believe in the same things that others seemed to, was to look around me at the religious.

They were all Christian. Christianity was everywhere—on every corner, down every street, on the backs of cars, on the ads in the telephone book—everywhere people proclaimed their belief in Christianity. I figured it must have some merit. I imagined that what was lacking was my knowledge of the Bible. Christians read it, no doubt, and not only understood it, but believed it. I had never read it. I did experience a few months in my early young adult years when I read parts of the New Testament and carried the Bible around like a child carries a doll, for comfort. I called myself Christian then as I had done all my life, but with more understanding of what it meant to be one; I prayed fervently for Christ to save me. Nothing happened; nothing changed in me. I eventually felt silly and stopped.

Now I read the Bible with keen interest. What was it about this book that caused people to believe in the god told of in it? In the Bible, I thought, I would find the answer; but I didn't. As I read the book, several things became apparent to me. First, it was obviously an ancient history, inaccurate and biased, and contained a great amount of mythology. Second, the god portrayed in the book was not as he was presented to me throughout my life. He was neither good nor loving, nor kind, just, forgiving, or merciful. Nothing about him resembled the god I thought of as the pinnacle of the Christian faith. I read the entire Old Testament and didn't find a good god anywhere in it.

Reading the Old Testament convinced me that I was an atheist, at least with regard to anthropomorphized gods such as Yahweh. It was in reading that book that I understood what humans do—they create gods and religions and philosophies to ease their fears of the unknown, to explain what they don't understand, to make themselves seem special and elite, and to set themselves apart from other tribes and cultures. I decided then that I wanted no part of any of that. I wanted only truth where I could find it. I would not believe something when there was no evidence backing it up. I didn't realize then how long it would take to achieve such a goal. I thought it would happen instantly; in a flash, I would rid myself of erroneous beliefs. Instead, they had to be shed like layers, one after the other over a period of time.

I stopped calling myself a Christian and became a Christian atheist. I'm serious. I held onto the Christian label because to disown it was a frightening prospect; not that I understood that consciously at the time. Certainly there could be nothing wrong with following such a great man as Jesus; a man so revered that millions of people thought he was no less than a god! But I hadn't yet finished the Bible. I still had the New Testament to read.

The New Testament was unfortunately jaded by the Old. I found nothing in it but a few snippets of kind words from a man who seemed to me to be rather arrogant and rude. I was disappointed to find that, again, I'd been lied to. Jesus wasn't the great spiritual leader I'd been told he was. While he did say some beautiful and noble things, he also said some ugly and cruel things. He didn't behave the way a loving teacher would—he was no Socrates.

I realized then that I couldn't call myself Christian anymore. I was a spiritual atheist because, though I didn't believe in the traditional idea of gods, I still believed that there could be something else, something greater than we are, and something more to life after our physical bodies die. Everyone around me believed in something—reincarnation, angels, a power greater than we are, and most importantly, some kind of eternal life. Though I could feel my beliefs slipping away, I wasn't ready to admit it; thinking consciously was something I learned gradually.

I closed the book that first summer of my unbelief without finding Christianity to be of any merit. I began to ask myself then, why do Christians believe what they do? Why do they see the Bible as something worthy of study? I felt a bit isolated and unsure of myself. I knew I didn't believe there was any spiritual truth behind the Bible but I wasn't sure that there wasn't something else to consider about Christianity.

I was on America Online at the time and was surprised and fascinated to find an atheist forum. It was wonderful to find that I wasn't alone, but I still had a need to understand why so many other people did believe in God. In the atheist forum, Christians infested the woodwork, darting out to damn us to Hell (most often in all capital letters) or ridicule our lack of understanding, only to scurry back into hiding; they never stayed around to hear our rebuttals.

I learned that there were other forums on the Internet where Christians actually engaged in debate with atheists and I was excited to find them and join in the arguing. For a year or two, I debated and found links to other sites and was recommended books on both atheism and Christian apologetics. A new world was opened up to me where I could begin to understand on what grounds Christians maintain their faith and on what grounds atheists reject it.

The first book I read on nonbelief was Dan Barker's *Losing Faith in Faith*. Next I read George Smith's *Atheism: The Case Against God*. Through these and many other books, I was finally guided toward rationalism and to an understanding of my own fears and bouts of illogic. Not everyone is born to think critically, that much is clear. I had to teach myself proper skepticism. How do I question, what do I question, what is logical, what is evidence? In the end, I found myself finally free of superstitious thinking and was proud to consider myself a rationalist.

I went through a pattern of phases with atheism, a generalized path that many other atheists may follow upon the realization of their nonbelief. First I experienced a period of confusion and sorting out of what exactly I believed or didn't believe. That was followed by a time of euphoria when a freedom overwhelmed me. This feeling wasn't like freedom from bondage. I wasn't celebrating the casting off of religion because I'd never really had it to begin with. It was a feeling of knowing myself, of the ability to be totally honest about who I was, at least with myself at first and then later, with others as well. This was, unfortunately, followed by a feeling of despair and loneliness when I found there weren't many others around like me. That was easy to overcome with the Internet sources available to me. A period of feeling angry and oppressed followed when I realized that Christians don't take too well to atheism. Eventually, I came out of it mellowed and settled happily into nonbelief.

I imagine that a second or third generation atheist wouldn't experience these problems. I can't say my parents are atheists; I can only say they aren't Christians. I wasn't indoctrinated with any theology as a child. Even when I believed in certain ideas, there was always the possibility in the back of my mind that I was wrong. I feel that I was most likely an atheist all along, but simply never had the opportunity or the gumption to address my assumptive beliefs sincerely until I gained enough self-esteem to handle it. I wasn't fully awake to myself and who I was. So, while I consider myself to have been an atheist all my life, it wasn't something I realized until adulthood. That realization caused me to be thrown into a pattern of withdrawal. For Christians who find themselves atheists, the pattern may be even more traumatic as an entire social group must be left behind or at least dealt with and years of indoctrination must be overcome.

It must be said that not all atheists make it through all the stages. I've met a couple who are still quite angry about their situations; I don't blame them. I've questioned many atheists. Some have expressed the same feelings I experienced but many others said they had no problem at all in realizing atheism; it was a natural step for them.

I believe it is a matter of self-esteem that determines how easily or difficult a person's transition will be. I lacked self-esteem and came to my realization of atheism as a part of gaining it. The two growth areas in my life were either entwined or parallel. As I became happier and more content in life and with my own being—as I became a friend to myself, trusted myself—I was able to question myself about the erroneous beliefs I maintained without reason.

Because of earlier bouts with low self-esteem, self-doubt crept in and caused this pattern of problems upon realizing atheism. If I had been a stronger person, I wouldn't have had the problems I had. But then, if I'd been a stronger person, I would have known all along I was atheist.

Attributing the atheist label to oneself can be a bit traumatic, especially for the weak-hearted like me. It's no wonder to me why so few actually do it. There must be thousands of people out there calling themselves agnostic, Humanist, rationalist, deist, pantheist, pagan, etc. who are, in actuality and when you get down to the core of their philosophies, atheists. But some would rather call themselves liberal Christians than atheists!

The term atheist represents, for a very vocal minority in this country, immorality, at best and at worst, Satanism (although I am referring to Satanism as defined by Biblical Christians). Atheism is despised by fundamentalist and conservative Christians. They fear it, I suppose. Looking at atheism is, after all, looking at the possibility that they are wrong. They must demonize atheism, because if they allow it some acceptance, it is liable to interfere with their faith. Without their faith they would be lost, hopeless, desperate, and according to those I've spoken with, immoral. It appears that they project their own fears onto those whose ideas frighten them. Because they would feel lost, hopeless, desperate and immoral without their beliefs, they assume that those who don't believe are, in fact, lost, desperate, hopeless and immoral.

It is, to many Christians, inconceivable that people can be happy, moral and well-adjusted without belief in deity. They seem to fear a society and a universe without the thought of some controlling force behind it. Everything must be directed by a power greater than they are because without that, they are merely tiny, insignificant creatures in a vast and impossible-to-understand universe. That frightens them; it scares them so much they are unwilling to even acknowledge the possibility that such a control doesn't exist. I can, honestly, understand that fear. It is perfectly natural as a human to fear the vast unknown, this world and universe that are so much larger than we are...and that feeling that we are on our own. The thought of such fear, in fact, helps us to understand why people created deity to begin with.

Not all Christians think atheists are unhappy and immoral. I've spoken with many who know that atheists are capable of happiness and morality just as Christians are. They may believe, though, that the happiness they have as Christians is deeper, more profound, and that their acts of morality glorify and please their god while the nonbeliever's conscience is just a happenstance of having been created with an infused sense of morality...by their god, of course.

Calling oneself atheist may be setting oneself up for hatred, intolerance, demonization, misunderstanding, and no small number of astonished looks from most of Christian society. Sometimes this isn't a problem. For the natural nonconformist, it's a normal day but for the average American, like me, it can be a difficult experience.

I always wanted to be liked. I wanted, more than anything as a youth, to be with the *in* group, the popular kids, the kids who socialized easily. They knew how to deal with people. I either never learned that, or I wasn't built that way. I spent my young adulthood and early married life trying to find a niche, a crowd to be *in*. When I peeled back the layers of myself to find the person at the center, I was at the same time proud and horrified at my discovery. Here I was, at the source of my self-ness, the real me. How many people traveled the road I did to find out who they really are? How many people were awake enough to do it? It was exhilarating, freeing, wondrous, and awesome. Suddenly the world was a magical place again, the universe open to all my questions.

Then it hit me—I'm the shunned. I'm the hated. One of my country's presidents (one I voted for!) said he didn't even consider me a citizen.[1] I'm the one they talk about in the Bible as wicked and always

---

[1] When campaigning for president, George Bush, Sr., during a press conference, said: "No, I don't know that Atheists should be considered as citizens, nor should they be considered patriots. This is one nation under God." You can read the entire exchange at *http://www.freethought-web.org/ctrl/news/file004.html* or search *www.freethought-web.org*.

lumped in with those who visit prostitutes for some reason. Damn, I thought, here I am again, and this time I'm farther toward the outer rim of society than ever! In school I could at least talk to the in-group. Now I was suddenly Satan. What is a rational girl to do?

My first goal was to learn why people believe that the Bible is anything more than historical fiction and why people believe that a man named Jesus really lived and rose from the dead. I wanted to understand why people seem religious by nature. When I learned enough to satisfy myself that Jesus probably never existed, I began a search to understand how a myth became thought of as historical fact. By what process did the story of Jesus, whether based on a real human or not, begin to be believed as if it were a historical event? When I finally had the answer to that question, Christianity began to make sense to me.

I've learned that there is no such thing as a true Christian or true Christianity. I've learned that religion fulfills certain basic human desires. Christians in particular and religious people in general have a different way of looking at the world than rationalists. Jesus was most likely a Jewish version of the popular pagan gods of that time. Christianity in its original form was quite pagan and mystical. Most important to me, I learned why I don't believe in, or even like, the Christian religion of today.

I am not a Satanist. I do not believe Satan exists. There are rational grounds for dismissing Christianity and a person needn't be in denial to do so. In order for me to freely accept others and their beliefs and allow that I have no power over what they believe, they must concede the same for me. Rationalists and religionists can coexist peacefully without having to belittle or demonize one another. The most important thing lacking in the relationship between the two is education. I have educated myself to a great extent about Christianity, its history, its philosophies, its dogma, and its adherents. This is my attempt to educate others, a little, about atheism.

Chapter Three

You Don't Say?

What do Christians think of atheism?

I've talked with many Christians, read their debates and arguments with others, shared letters with them via email and while I can't say that I know how every Christian thinks, I can offer you a sampling of what I have heard from the Christian teachers I've had the pleasure of interacting with.

"There aren't any atheists"

Some Christians don't believe there are any real atheists. They say that atheists know, deep down, that there is a god. God, they say, is evident in all creation. They quote Paul in Romans 1, which says,

> The wrath of God is indeed being revealed from Heaven against every impiety and wickedness of those who suppress the truth by their wickedness. For what can be known about God is evident to them because God made it evident to them. Ever since the creation of the world, his invisible attributes of eternal power and divinity have been able to be understood and perceived in what he has made. As a result, they have no excuse; for although they knew God they did not accord him glory as God or give him thanks. Instead, they became vain in their reasoning, and their senseless minds were darkened. While claiming to be wise, they became fools and exchanged

the glory of the immortal God for the likeness of an image of mortal man or of birds or of four-legged animals or of snakes.

(Romans 1: 18-23)

Obviously, many people very early on didn't believe in the Christian message and Paul felt it necessary to defend his faith. According to Paul, everything that we need to know to know God exists has been made evident to us and we suppress this truth because of our wickedness. While the verses are specific to paganism, I can see how they can be applied to nonbelief as well. One might question in what manner the wrath of God is being revealed against the wickedness of us nonbelievers; I haven't noticed anything. One might also question the worship of the mortal man Jesus in light of Paul's words. Most importantly, one should recognize that all the writings of Paul and others defending their religious views are propaganda for the faith. Men often make false accusations regarding the "enemy" to bolster their own positions.

Christians say atheists know as well as they do that God exists; we just deny him because we're evil. This, as you can guess, is not a very good way to approach an atheist. The odd thing is that once an atheist is offered this rather cruel opinion and dares to exhibit anger, the Christian is likely to point the finger at him and cry, "Aha! You're angry at God!"

"Atheists are angry at God"

The "angry at God" accusation usually takes the form of "something bad must have happened to you to cause you to turn away from God." Anything unfavorable that may have befallen the atheist is brought up as a possibility for the poor soul's rash decision to turn from God: the loss of a parent, child or loved one; poverty or loss of income; legal problems; poor health or disease. It has even been suggested that because God does not answer my prayers in the manner I would wish, I am angry at him.

No matter how the atheist protests that he simply doesn't believe and that he can't be angry with an entity that doesn't exist, the Christian continues to claim it is merely anger at God or at his own life circumstance that causes the atheist's disbelief. It can be quite maddening.

"Atheists hate God"

Related to the "angry at God" accusation is the claim that the atheist hates God. The atheist, for whatever reason whether it be the actions of God as described in the Old Testament, the death of a loved one, evil on Earth, or simply a hardened heart, has a deep hatred for the loving Christian god.

Why, beyond Paul's assumption, do you suppose that Christians must continue to claim that everyone knows God exists and anyone who denies it must be troubled? If I tried to put myself in Christian shoes, I might be able to understand. Christians believe in something...they believe it with all their hearts and minds; at least they try to. This god of theirs is not clearly evident; he is subtle, works in mysterious ways, they experience him subjectively. When someone comes along and claims they believe in something that isn't there...I can imagine it doesn't feel good to hear it. But, it is wrong to turn our own discomfort onto others by assuming we know what they think, feel and believe better than they do.

Christians must accept that atheists simply *do not believe it*. I have found that the more secure a Christian is in his own belief, the easier it is for him to accept simple nonbelief. People who are angry at or hate God can't be atheists because atheists don't believe a god exists.

"Atheism is a choice"

Some Christians claim that atheists are such because they want to be—they choose to disbelieve in God because they do not want to live their lives according to his will. We want to be our own gods, they say; we want no authority over our lives save our own. Many will go so far as to claim that we want to live immoral lives. The immorality is almost always sexual; at least, no one has yet accused me of wanting to steal or murder...just sleep around. Although, it has been argued that without a god, there is nothing to stop me from murdering...but we'll get to morality later.

Perhaps it is a desire for agreement from others that causes believers to say these things about nonbelievers. Or perhaps they believe that the only reason they themselves are moral people is because they worship a god; so anyone who doesn't couldn't possibly be good. Atheists are normal people just like Christians. We aren't thieves, murderers, or rapists, at least, no more often than are Christians comparatively speaking.

I've been accused of wanting to be my own god—that atheists worship themselves—but, gods are supernatural beings, so that would be absurd. However, the Christian attempts to get around this by claiming that anything that a person worships is like a god. But, "like a god" and "actually a god" are different. The point in the assertion is that atheists worship something other than God. "Everyone worships *something*," I've been told. This is mere projection; an insistence that because they worship something, everyone else does also. I do not worship *anything*. I do not bow down to any idol, being, emotion, physical object, or monetary unit and praise it. I don't worship myself; I don't live my life as a hedonist by any means. I am a normal person just like most Christians...except that they believe in a god and I do not.

The point also is to claim that atheists resist authority. Yet, atheists are law abiding citizens as often as are Christians. We recognize and respect the authorities we have elected to govern our society. Atheists simply don't believe that there is a god exercising authority over mankind. In fact, it's rather clear to us that there is not because God's supposed authority only comes into play after we die. Here on Earth, so-called free will reigns. God, if he has authority, doesn't exercise it. He doesn't punish the thief, the murderer, or the rapist...we do. Apparently, he won't punish the criminal even after death if he repents and turns his life over to Jesus before he expires. Atheists don't want to resist a god's authority; we don't believe that a god exists.

We don't choose our beliefs. We either believe something or we don't. People can't choose to believe God exists any more than they can choose to believe he doesn't. Atheism isn't a choice; it's a label.

"Atheists deny God"

Christians often make the claim that atheists deny their god. They do this because it is a subtle reinforcement of their own beliefs. God is real, to the Christian, and anyone who claims otherwise is simply denying God and God's will.

A person can't deny someone who doesn't exist. Gilligan, the one on the island, does not exist. My saying he does not exist is in no way denying Gilligan. My father, on the other hand, exists. If I claim he doesn't, I am denying my father. There is a difference. I can very much understand the Christian claim that atheists deny God because they believe it is a point of fact that their god exists. In order for them to understand atheists, however, and to be able to engage in discourse with them, Christians must accept that for the atheist, the question of a god's existence is not decided. It is debatable. There is no evidence beyond the subjective experiences, feelings, and desires of other humans to offer on the pro side. The atheist is quite within the realm of logic in his rejection of the claim of a god's existence and the Christian should kindly respect the atheist's lack of belief. Atheists do not deny God because, until proven otherwise, God is a fictional character.

"Atheists worship Satan"

There's no arguing with a person who believes that atheists worship Satan. Naturally, the atheist response is that we can't worship an entity we don't believe exists; but the problem is that the Christian who believes we worship Satan will claim that we don't know we're doing it. Satan has blinded us to the truth of Christianity and to the truth of his own existence as well. We worship him because he controls us and we do his bidding, presumably by turning innocent Christians into atheists or insulting God, without realizing we're doing it. We wouldn't be susceptible to Satan if we'd turn to God.

There's just no arguing with that. But, I suppose one might ask...how do you know? How do you know when Satan has control over you and when God does? How do you know that Christianity isn't Satan's ploy to lure Jews away from the truth of God? You don't.

If I can be blinded by Satan so much that I am convinced that I don't believe something I supposedly really do, or even that Satan himself doesn't exist, then how could God be more powerful than Satan? How can God allow Satan to blind people so? The Christian tells me that it is my sinful human state that allows it. In other words, I allow Satan to convince me that neither Satan nor God exists. This seems silly to me. Why would God create me without the ability to resist Satan? Why would he allow Satan to continue with such a ruse?

If it is possible for Satan to so convince me of a lie, then it is equally possible that Satan is deceiving Christians. Maybe Satan has turned Christians away from the true nature of God. Maybe Satan inspired the Bible and not God. Or maybe, as is possible to believe after a good reading of the Old Testament, God is the bad guy and Satan is the good guy.

It really doesn't matter to me. I don't believe either of them exists.

"Atheists have no purpose in their lives"

Christians sometimes think that atheists have no purpose in their lives because they don't believe in an eternal life or in a creator. I can understand this difficulty. To some, the thought that this life is all we have is frightening and sad but, it isn't for all of us. I can't explain why that is; perhaps it's genetic. I do know, however, that I am not bothered by a finite lifetime. In fact, I have considered the idea of eternal life and I am not thrilled by it. I don't find the idea at all appealing. I wouldn't mind living for a few thousand years I suppose, but not much beyond that. As Susan Ertz said, "Millions long for immortality who don't know what to do on a rainy Sunday afternoon." (From *Brainy-Quote.com*)

Christians have told me that their purpose is to glorify their god. Without that purpose, the human has no reason for being. Naturally an atheist wouldn't accept this claim. That kind of purpose is meaningless to me. I don't see any design for human life in general. We are a highly evolved species, here, not because of the guiding hand of a deity-creator, but through the evolutionary processes that resulted in life on this planet. Life is, in essence, without purpose; but not having an ultimate reason for being doesn't affect the everyday lives of humans.

Atheists have purpose in their lives in the same way believers do. We find meaning in daily living, joy in our hobbies, satisfaction in doing a job well, or enjoyment of spending the money our jobs earn. Atheist parents experience the same joy in raising their children as Christians do. Our hearts fill with love and pride at our children's first smiles and steps in the same way theirs do. Purpose in life for atheists is very much the same as for Christians. The atheist even goes beyond that to a grander, larger purpose: that of our descendants. Atheists are part of those who work for a better tomorrow, a cleaner, healthier Earth, for scientific and medical research to improve the lives of those who will come after us. But atheists don't go farther than that to a supernatural, or eternal, purpose. We don't need one.

"Atheists are depressed and hopeless"

Ah, Nietzsche, the anvil you've laid on our backs! Nietzsche was a great philosopher and thinker; his works are still influential today. But yes, he went mad from syphilis and died insane. Whenever anyone wants to claim that atheists are depressed and bound to end up crazy, they point to poor Nietzsche as if he was the epitome of atheism. He is not. Why do you suppose they are always pointing to Nietzsche? Because he's an easy target.

I've been told that atheists are depressed, hopeless people. I have found that to be untrue. I've been fortunate enough to meet many atheists. I was thrilled to join hundreds at a convention of American Atheists in 2001. I proudly joined thousands in the first Godless Americans March on Washington on November 2, 2002. I attended an awe-inspiring convention hosted by Atheist Alliance International and heard fabulous speakers at the national convention of the Freedom From Religion Foundation, both in 2003. I will continue to attend such meetings in the future.

Through my website at *www.atheistview.com*, and in reading the many sites published by atheists, I enjoy hearing from other nonbelievers. There are local groups of atheists in most communities, just as there are in mine. So far, the atheists I've met and corresponded with have been normal, joyful, intelligent people. Atheists suffer no more from depression than do Christians.

I can understand the fear and sadness many may feel when they contemplate the fact that this life must end, but I don't believe that Christians think about death every minute of the day. I don't think they think about it any more often than atheists...and that isn't very often. Why would the atheist be overpowered with sadness simply by occasionally considering the fact that he will cease to exist? It's a fact of life. It comes across my mind sometimes, but I don't fear it—it doesn't overwhelm me.

Atheists grow and learn, just like Christians do. They forge bonds with family and friends, fall in love, marry, and raise, even homeschool, well-adjusted children. They teach others, help others, and care for others, just like Christians do. The only difference is that for some reason, maybe Christians have a deeper need to feel safe and secure than atheists. Or maybe atheists have that need also, but we are just able to accept what we perceive as our reality regardless of our feelings about it.

"Atheism is a religion"

Religion is a belief in or reverence for supernatural powers, like gods. The word also refers to particular systems of belief. Does that sound like atheism at all? Atheism is lack of belief in deity. Deities are super-natural entities. The atheist does not believe in such, have reverence for, nor worship such. Atheism is not a religion. It's a description.

The only definition that might be construed in such a way as to make atheism into a religion is that of religious passion—a cause, prin-ciple or activity pursued with zeal. This still doesn't speak of atheism, however, because atheism isn't a cause, principle or activity. Separa-tion of church and state is a cause. A lack of belief in something is not a cause. "Do only good" could be a principle. Lack of belief in some-thing is not. Speaking out against prayer in school is an activity; lack of belief in something is not.

The best you can say is that some atheists have philosophies of life that they pursue with a passion, call it religious, if you like. You could say that some atheists protest government intrusion into our lives with religious zeal. But you can't say that atheism itself is a religion. Athe-ism does not speak to the individual atheist's beliefs, only to his lack of belief in deity.

Why try to call atheism a religion? Theists are always trying to make atheism into something it is not in order to attack it more easily. The as-sertion that atheism is a religion is an attempt to make atheism into a positive claim, instead of a lack of belief. That way, the Christian can try to force the atheist to support his supposed positive claim that there is no god. But atheism is not a religion, it is not a belief. There is no positive claim. It is, clearly, the theists who claim that something not evident ex-ists and they have the burden of proof on their shoulders. Until they admit this fact, there will be problems between our two camps, because trying to make atheism into something it is not to avoid the fact that there is no proof or valid evidence to offer for god is disingenuous.

Even strong atheists who claim that god does not exist do not have the burden of proof. Claiming god does not exist is not a positive claim; it is a denial of the theist's positive claim. Look at it this way: I believe that *Gone with the Wind* is historically factual and Scarlett O'Hara ex-isted as a real person. You say: Scarlett O'Hara is a fictional character; she does not exist. Who has the burden of proof? I do. This is no differ-ent than the theist/atheist debate in which believers point to a book of stories, the Bible, claim it is historically factual and that Yahweh, a character in the stories, exists as a real entity. I say: Yahweh is a fic-tional character; he does not exist. Who has the burden of proof? Believers do.

I am not asking Christians to admit that atheism is correct, or that Christianity is wrong. I only ask that they accept atheism for what it is: simple nonbelief in gods—and allow that the atheist and the theist have different ideas about what constitutes evidence.

"Atheists are close-minded"

This, above all, is the most perplexing comment hurled at me in discussions with Christians. What does it mean to be close-minded? It sometimes seems as if, to the Christian, a close-minded person is anyone who disagrees with his dogma. I admit that isn't always the case with every Christian I have come across. One told me that I am close-minded to the spiritual realm, to subjective experience as evidence for deity. This is still not true of me. I have had subjective experiences that have encouraged me to explore ideas beyond the reality that rationalism makes evident to me but, because I have no evidence thus far that these experiences are anything beyond normal human phenomena, I do not give them any special weight in determining truth and reality.

As to the spiritual realm, I don't have any experience of such a realm. I have never interpreted any feeling of mine as communication from gods, demons, angels, or any other supernatural being; as far as I know, no otherworldly creature has interacted with me or possessed my body or that of anyone I know. When I believed in a Universal Mind, I often felt that profound "oneness" with existence on contemplating love or being. It was a tingly, filled-up sensation. I felt I was more than just my physical body. Many people experience this and interpret it in various ways. For the Christian it is being filled with a holy spirit. For me, it was being at one with existence. As a rationalist, I see it as a deep awareness of my reality. I experience the same thing I did before...I merely interpret it differently now. I am not close-minded to subjective experience. Simply show me some evidence linking it to a god or a supernatural realm and I'll make a judgment.

What is close-minded? A person is close-minded when he refuses to examine evidence, accept facts, or thoughtfully consider an opposing view. Close-mindedness is adhering to a dogma—a set of principles that must be believed. I am not that person. I am willing to look at any evidence presented to me of views that I do not hold. I have no dogma to adhere to that would prevent me from accepting facts and evidence at odds with it.

But, I am a rationalist and I use my reason first to determine truth. Reason tells me that there are no gods, the Bible god can not exist, and that Christianity is not true. I must filter any evidence you offer me for your beliefs through my reason. I am more than willing to do so...I have done so. I am still atheist; not because of a refusal to believe (that would be close-minded) but because the evidence is lacking.

I have been told that atheism is just as dogmatic as Christianity. How so? There is no dogma attached to atheism. Atheism says nothing about what one must believe...only a description of one thing a person does not believe. Many Christians say that the atheist dogma insists atheists believe in or accept the following: evolution, reason and science above subjective experience, anti-religion, pro-abortion, and the Democratic Party. This is absurd. I have met Republican atheists; I was one. There are atheists on both sides and in between on the abortion issue; some atheists are very into the supernatural, not all are against religion by any means and not all atheists are convinced of the facts of evolutionary theories.

Assuming anything about atheists beyond their lack of belief in deity tells them that you aren't listening to them, that you haven't thought about the label or worse, that you are trying to make them into something they're not in order to attack them.

So, what do atheists "believe?"

I once visited a Church of Religious Science where I thought I would meet people who could at least understand atheism. After the service I was approached by a big-haired woman who wanted to know what brought me to her church that day. I told her a bit about myself and mentioned that I was an atheist. The first words out of her mouth were "everyone believes in something."

What does that mean exactly? Isn't that just another feel-good phrase that helps people feel secure? Everyone believes in something, so it's alright if I believe this thing, strange as it may seem to others. I was put off by her remark. I felt she was making a claim that I could not be atheist...it wasn't acceptable to her. I don't believe that everyone has to believe in something.

Christians tell me that everyone has faith in something. First, we'd have to define faith. Faith means different things. Faith in common usage means confidence in something, someone, or some idea. Faith in the religious sense can mean belief that doesn't rest on logical proof or physical evidence, the virtue of having faith, or a religion itself.

With the first definition in mind, yes, I as an atheist do have faith in some things like my husband and family—that is a confidence and trust in them. But that's not what Christians mean when they tell me I have faith in things in the same way they have faith in their god. I'm not saying they don't experience feelings of confidence and trust in their god; certainly they do. I'm saying that they are trying to equate that kind of faith with the faith that is belief without evidence. I don't have any belief without evidence...in anything.

I've been told that I must have faith or I couldn't live. Every morning, I have faith the Sun will rise. Every time I dare to cross the street I exercise my faith that I won't be hit by a car. I am told that this is faith, indeed, and it is the same as having faith that Jesus rose from the dead. I don't agree.

I don't know that the Sun will rise tomorrow but, it has risen every morning of my life. I understand how the Earth works, how it spins around giving me the illusion that the Sun rises and sets. I understand that one day far in the future the Sun will burn out and about eight minutes later, the Earth will be in darkness. My experience has taught me that the Sun will rise tomorrow. I don't have faith in the Sun's rising. I don't *believe* it will rise. I expect it to, based on evidence and experience.

I don't know that I won't be hit by a car crossing the street. I don't have faith when I cross. I don't say a little prayer before stepping off the curb. I use my knowledge of cars and speed to determine the best course of action. My experience with heavy objects and in reading about people being hit by cars and the fear that arises when I consider such stories brings me caution. I don't use faith to cross the street. If I used faith, I'd just step off the curb whenever and have a go, but instead, I use my knowledge and experience to cross the street and do my best to avoid harm.

Faith, in the religious sense, is harmful. Faith (belief that doesn't rest on logical proof or material evidence) can be dangerous. Believing in something without evidence leaves a person open to belief in all sorts of nonsense; it takes scientific, logical evaluation out of the equation; it allows humanity to continue to deny its reality and finite nature; it hinders progress.

Faith is often tied to dogma and dogma is dangerous. Dogma allows some people to control or hate masses of others. Dogma closes the mind to inquiry and doubt, the things from which creativity, science and discovery arise.

Granted, there are those who have faith in gods, nature spirits, and afterlife who have no dogma ruling their beliefs, but I think that a society rooted in rationalism would be a far better one than a society based in a supernatural realm for which there is no evidence.

But, what do atheists believe? That depends on the atheist. Some atheists believe in life on other planets, that life on Earth was purposefully spawned from life on another world, that aliens came to this Earth long ago and ancient man drew pictures of them on cave walls, that crop circles are supernaturally or alien made, that the stars and their placement at the time of your birth can determine your personality and events in your future, or that after we die we are reborn as a more enlightened individual, or as an animal. There are all sorts of people in this world who don't believe in gods, but believe in other equally indefensible propositions.

The atheists that I am acquainted with, however, tend to be rationalists. Rationalism, as a philosophy, asserts that reason, not subjective experience, authority of any sort—man or book—or spiritual revelation, is the *primary* basis for knowledge and should be used to determine reality. Rationalism leads to atheism. All rationalists are atheists (Thomas Paine notwithstanding; he claimed that rationalism leads to deism, an opinion I dispute). But, and this is very important, all atheists are not rationalists. Rationalists don't *believe in* anything.

Belief versus knowledge

Christians have often asked me how I can believe in nothing. It has been difficult to pin down their exact meaning. It is not true that I believe in nothing. *Nothing* is not something one can believe in, because it is...*nothing*. It is not that I *believe in* nothing but that I don't *believe in* anything. There is a difference.

What does it mean to believe in something? As with faith, the term belief has a variety of meanings. When we believe in a proposition, we hold it to be true. Does truth require belief? Solipsism aside, we must accept that there are many things we can hold to be true and factual. That we exist and our reality is as we objectively perceive it can be taken as fact (in other words, we can reasonably assume we aren't dreaming this existence nor are we just brains in jars, or batteries in tubs of goo as in *The Matrix*).

There is truth to be had and we don't have to believe in it. We believe in those things for which we can't know the facts or the truth. We believe in things we don't know for certain. Dan Barker illustrated this point humorously in his book, *Losing Faith in Faith* (FFRF, Inc. 1992):

> Truth does not have to be believed. Scientists do not join hands every Sunday, singing, "Yes, gravity is real! I will have faith! I will be strong! I believe in my heart that what goes up, up, up must come down, down, down. Amen!" If they did, we would think they were pretty insecure about it.

Truth doesn't require belief. Nor does it require defense; it can stand on its own. Rationalists look for factual, objective evidence. If none can be had, we remain without an answer; we do not create a belief in order to have one. When you know something to be true, you don't have to believe in it.

And that is why people must believe in God. They don't know that he is there. If they knew it, belief and faith would be unnecessary. If God could be objectively perceived, making it possible for his existence to be known, we would all know it. In that respect, the mere fact that the debate over God's existence occurs is evidence that *he* does not.

I don't believe in anything because I don't want to create a belief where I can't have a truth. I am more comfortable without an answer than with a belief that could be false.

Chapter Four

There's No Such Thing as a True Christian

No man ever believes that the Bible means what it says: He is always convinced that it says what he means.

—George Bernard Shaw

What is a Christian?

I've learned a great deal by talking to and debating with Christians. One thing I learned is that they are all very different. I have had the opportunity of discussing faith with a variety of believers in many different forums. I've found that there are all sorts of Christians. There are Christians who believe that Jesus was a prophet, not the one and only son of God. There are those who do not believe the Bible is the word of God but writings of fallible men. There are those who believe that the Bible, when interpreted correctly, is a symbolic story of salvation, and Jesus is our savior only in that he was the only human in history to come as close to awareness of the god in all of us. Then, there are those Christians who believe that every word in the Bible is utter Truth (with a capital T).

Most of those who believe that the Bible is true and inerrant have probably never read it. Those who have, and have studied Biblical inerrancy, have very interesting methods of interpreting it so that it is not, in fact, contradictory or error-prone at all. They call on all sorts of techniques from literary style, comparative understanding of words, to determining the nature of Jesus and then interpreting everything he said according to what he must have meant or what the text must mean according to what they claim to know regarding Jesus' intentions. With those sorts of Christians, for example, hate doesn't mean hate; it must mean "to love less."

I agree that not all of the problems that skeptics point out in the Bible are unexplainable. A few of them are understandable when read without the determination to find fault with the text. A small number of them are understandable when interpreted with literary style, cultural differences and symbolism taken into account but that doesn't leave the Bible free of contradiction and error; it hardly lessens the problems with the book at all. There are contradictions in the Bible—blatant ones that can't be argued away.

Did God create man before the animals (Gen 2:18-20) or after (Gen 1:25, 26)? Did God order a census (2Sam 24:1) or did Satan (1Chron 21:1)? Is wisdom good (Prov 4:7; Prov 3:13) or bad (1Cor 1:19)? Is the god of the Bible peaceful (Rom 15:33)? A god of love (1John 4:8)? Or is he a god of war (Exod 15:3)? And vengeful (Nah 1:2)?

Christians run the gamut from the inerrancy group to the most liberal quasi-Christians you may find in a Unity Church. They all adhere to the teachings of Jesus as they understand them. They all interpret the meaning of the word Christ as they see fit. They all interpret the Bible correctly according to themselves and they all lead their lives according to their own personal choices in the matter.

There really isn't any such thing as a true Christian. Every Christian I've talked to, from the screaming (typing in all-caps on the Internet is considered yelling) lunatic on line to the friendly neighborhood church-goer, told me he was a true Christian—the real thing. Usually this statement was made to separate the true from the false who, they assured me, was the type I had run into in the past.

The more liberal or progressive the Christian, the less likely he is to claim that other Christians are false; that nonbelievers, followers of other faiths, and other Christians will suffer in a place called Hell after this life on Earth; that God prescribes a strict moral code for our lives; that theories of evolution are false and that there is only one true path to salvation, that being through Jesus Christ. The more liberal the Christian, the more tolerant and loving he tends to be.

Needless to say, many of the Christians I refer to in this book are not, by any means, the most liberal. I have little problem with Universalists who believe that we are all children of the divine and that when this life is over, we will rejoin that divine parent. I don't accept their theology, nor their assumptions and presuppositions, or their methods of determining truth. But while their beliefs contradict science and rationalism, they are, for the most part, leaving me alone.

I do have a problem with Christians who believe the Bible is the unchanging word of their god. They tend to want to enforce their version of Biblical morality on the rest of society and establish a Christian theocracy in this country. Unfortunately, there seem to be too many Christians willing to go along with this supposed minority of vocal and extreme Biblicists, because they're Christians too, after all, and what harm can there be in the Bible?

What is Christianity anyway? If all Christians believe that they are true Christians and they all believe that they have it right—the right interpretation of scripture, the right viewpoint, the right moral code, the right church—then how do we know which are true and which aren't? If they're all correct, how can they be so different?

Some Christians tell me that all the Christian denominations aren't that much different. They all agree on certain basic principles. Most of the traditional Protestant churches agree on certain ideas like, Jesus is the son of God and he was crucified and rose again. That's pretty much a must that you have to believe if you want to be a Christian, right? Not according to what I've learned. Some believe that Jesus is God. Some believe he was a man. Some say he was both God and a man. Some churches believe that there are three gods in one: Father, Son and Holy Spirit. Others believe there is only one god. Some venerate Mary; others consider that a desperate sin. Some believe that salvation is gained by faith which leads to works; others by faith alone; others by works alone; others by works *and* faith. And some believe that neither will get you eternal life as only God can bestow it by grace. The problem is that Christians can easily claim that all true Christians think and believe pretty much the same by simply asserting that anyone who doesn't believe that way, isn't a true Christian.

The best answer I ever received about what a true Christian is was on an email list created for the express purpose of asking and answering questions about Christianity. A true Christian, the moderator told me, is a person who believes that Jesus Christ is his personal savior. At the very least, a Christian must be a follower of the teachings of Jesus, be he man or god. This is what I understand to be the case but when cornered, when pinned down to explain point by point what these teachings of Jesus are, for some strange reason, Christians end the conversation.

What did Jesus teach?

I would have said, long ago, when I thought Jesus was a great moral teacher as he is still purported to be, that "love one another" was one of Jesus' basic teachings. But was it? Jesus taught in parables, stories that have a deeper meaning. In his stories we can glean the ideas of caring for the poor and sick, living humbly, and forgiving others. Jesus said to the rich man that to get into Heaven he must: not kill, not commit adultery, not steal, not bear false witness, honor your father and mother and love your neighbor as yourself. (Matt 19:16-19) These are all very good things to strive for (unless you've been abused by your parents, of course). It is easy to see why people would concentrate on these good teachings that Jesus supposedly gave us.

If we look closer at the gospels, however, we read that not everything Jesus told us to do was good and not every sentiment spoken by him was what I would expect from a loving god, his son, or even a wise prophet. Consider the parable of the ten gold coins. This is a fine story about God, or Jesus, entrusting his followers with spiritual gifts or talents, to be used to better the world, themselves, or, God's kingdom. The servant who buries his talent, however, is punished; his talent is taken from him. This makes good sense. Make the most of your gifts; if you hide your talents, they are worthless and you may lose them. It's what Jesus said in the end of the story that bothers me. Speaking as the one who gave his servants coins (that would be God or Jesus), he said, "Now for those enemies of mine who did not want me as their king, bring them here and slay them before me." (Luke 19:27) What did he mean by that except that the master (God or Jesus) would have killed those who don't worship him? That doesn't sound like the actions of a loving god to me. It isn't the sort of language befitting a great teacher. Would a loving god who desires a relationship with its creation use threats of death to gain it?

In Jesus' explanation of the parable of the weeds among the wheat in Matthew 13, he claimed that there are evil ones, those who cause others to sin and sin themselves, children of the devil. At some point in the future, harvest time, the angels "will throw them into the fiery furnace, where there will be wailing and grinding of teeth." I have a hard time understanding this theory of a loving god versus an evil god. In the end, the loving god will triumph by torturing the evil god and his followers in a fiery furnace. Not only does it sound magical and fictional, it is so obviously divisive that it has caused many to claim self-righteous superiority over others by simply labeling their enemies as children of the devil...exactly the way many Christians deal with atheists. This doesn't sound like a god of love to me.

Jesus said that spreading the gospel of God would cause problems for his disciples. The word of the loving, benevolent father/god will cause a lot of people to get very mean with Christians. This could be explained by the actions of sinful Adam damning all of us and making us so unworthy that hearing the good news about God will make most of us really pissed off.

Jesus admitted that he was divisive when he said:

> Do not think that I have come to bring peace upon the earth. I have come to bring not peace but the sword. For I have come to set a man against his father, a daughter against her mother and a daughter-in-law against her mother-in-law; and one's enemies will be those of his household. (Matt. 10:34-36)

I guess that I would have to first agree that man is inherently evil, sinful and unworthy before I could accept this as good news. Jesus was saying that people are going to hate you for what you say and do. But hey, that's God's word and it's going to cause a lot of problems because it's so good and loving and merciful and kind. Only if humans are so ensconced in evil, could goodness, love, mercy, and kindness cause division in households. I don't accept that view of humanity. The fact that Jesus did causes me some pause. But Jesus' words are understandable; when you preach condemnation for others, you ought to expect some flack.

In what way is it good that a person can't follow Jesus unless he hates his mother and father, wife and children, brothers and sisters, and even his own life (Luke 14:26), especially considering that would be going against one of the commandments Jesus claimed in Matthew 19. I have heard only one explanation for that particular problem: Jesus didn't mean hate; he meant "love less than me." I appreciate the need to make things better but, frankly, if Jesus didn't mean hate, why is the word hate in the verse? The only way out of this predicament is to say that Jesus would not have said such a thing so it can't possibly mean what it says.

If the Bible, the word of the one and only God, doesn't mean what it says, how can we take any of it as truth? If we can reinterpret different parts of it and claim that the words themselves can't be defined by normal, daily usage, we are left with a book that can't be trusted. We are left at the mercy of others to tell us what it means. We are left in the hands of fallible men.

What Jesus didn't say is as important as what he did. He never spoke out against slavery; in fact, he seemed to be okay with it. Jesus clarified a parable by describing the beating of servants as if it was of no consequence (Luke 12:47, 48). That hardly sounds loving, gentle, merciful and kind.

Though Jesus said a few good things, he wasn't, when objectively viewed, a loving teacher. He treated his disciples with contempt for human failures, like their inability to understand the meaning behind his convoluted parables, and their inability to believe the impossible, like his walking on water. He also treated his mother and siblings with rudeness; he didn't follow his own commandment to respect his mother.

The worst thing Jesus did was to forever cause hatred, war, slaughter, burnings, and divisiveness among humanity when he said, "Whoever is not with me is against me..." (Matt 12:30). That must be true, considering he taught "whoever does not believe [in him] has already been condemned, because he has not believed in the name of the only son of God" (John 3:18). I suppose it's just me, but I don't see condemnation, hatred and Hell being related in any way to an all-loving deity.

On the other hand, if we look at the possibility that Jesus didn't exist, that he was a construct of the Jewish pagans and the gospel stories were written during varying times of oppression of the Jews, the words attributed to Jesus begin to make more sense. When we look at them as written by the persecuted, as propaganda for a cause, they are more understandable.

Do Christians follow Jesus' teachings?

Christianity is clearly based on the person of Jesus Christ. As the Christ, Jesus is the savior of mankind and the world. His teachings are quoted in the gospels; we are to assume his words are correctly attributed to him and are true. Jesus' words then, above any other person's in the Bible, are sacred.

Jesus offered his followers precepts that seem rather tough to live by; and certainly many, if not most, of the Christians I meet aren't abiding by his words. There are some glaring differences between Jesus' teachings and the Christian churches' today.

The most important difference regards the Old Testament laws which Jesus said he didn't intend to abolish. He said if you didn't maintain the law better than the Scribes and Pharisees you were in danger of punishment (Matt 5:17-20). But no Christian today follows those old laws. Perhaps the problem is that in other parts of the gospels, Jesus contradicts himself by amending some of those older laws. If I were a Christian, I would accept amendments to the law only in those instances where Jesus said it was allowable and I would not consider any of the laws abolished.

According to Jesus, not only can't you kill, but you can't even be angry. If you call someone a fool, you're in trouble. (Then of course, Jesus went on to call a few people fools in Matt. 23:17.)

Not only can you not commit adultery, but you can't even look at a woman with lust because when you do, you've committed adultery in your heart. If you are prone to leering, you must pluck out your eye. I don't know why Christians try to say Jesus didn't really mean for you to pluck out your eyes when he said it pretty clearly: pluck out the offending member to save your soul (Matt 5:29).

The Old Testament law said you could divorce your wife but Jesus said doing so would make her guilty of adultery. Anyone who marries a divorced woman is committing adultery. Any man who divorces his wife and marries another woman commits adultery. All divorced Christian women, all men who have married previously-married women, and all men married more than once are adulterers. The penalty for adultery is death (Lev. 20:10).

Jesus also said to "offer no resistance to one who is evil" then went on to talk about people hitting you and asking you to walk with them. You aren't supposed to resist mean people; you're supposed to let them have at you. Offer them your other cheek to slap. Walk not one mile with the slave driver but two. When someone asks you for something that belongs to you, hand it over. I don't know any Christians who live this way.

Jesus said to "be perfect, just as your Heavenly Father is perfect." (Matt 5:48) And yet, I always see bumper stickers that say, "Christians aren't perfect, just forgiven." Jesus told his followers to be perfect; if they're not, then they're not very good Christians, are they?

Jesus said not to let people see you doing good deeds just so you get rewarded; I guess you're supposed to be modest. And he said not to pray like hypocrites pray, standing in synagogues and on the street. You're supposed to go to your inner room and close the door. Jesus also said not to babble when you pray like the pagans do because God already knows what you want before you open your mouth. Go to your closet and pray with your mouth shut. Funny, I hear all about the "see you at the pole" prayers at schools; our government representatives pray all the time in public meetings before they do their jobs. I've witnessed parishioners in churches praying out loud, their hands upraised, dancing and praising God; on television they really go at it. That doesn't seem to be what Jesus wants them to do.

You're not supposed to shore up treasures on Earth. You shouldn't accumulate jewels and expensive collections and such. Jesus said that no one can serve two masters and that therefore you shouldn't worry about your life, what you'll eat, drink, or wear. God will fulfill your needs. Naturally Christians aren't going to follow this tenet. If they did, they'd be beggars and homeless people. God said he'd provide, but he doesn't really so they have to get jobs and accumulate some wealth. If Christians really just let God provide and he actually did, they might have some evidence for the validity of their religion.

Christians are to stop judging others—that would include me, I suppose. In the manner that they judge others, they too will be judged. But, so many Christians are so judgmental! They are so quick to tell us who is bad and who is good, who is a true Christian and who is not. I guess any Christian that passes judgment on anyone else isn't a true Christian.

Right after Jesus said not to judge people, he told Christians not to "give what is holy to dogs, or throw your pearls before swine, lest they trample them underfoot, and turn and tear you to pieces." (Matt 7:6) If he wasn't really talking about dogs and swine there, wasn't he making an awful judgment about certain people and calling Christians to do so as well?

I've been told that even though Jesus clearly said, "Do not judge," he didn't mean it. He actually taught how to *discern* between the good and bad people. That's a slippery evasion if I ever heard one. "Do not judge" actually means "here's how to judge." Sure, sure. Apparently the rules can be played with so that Christians can behave the way they want, regardless of what Jesus said, and still count themselves among the elect.

The most glaring denial of Jesus' teachings is about wealth. Jesus said to the rich man: "If you wish to be perfect [which according to his own words you are supposed to be], go, sell what you have and give to the poor." (Matt 19: 21) He told everyone that it is very difficult for rich people to get into Heaven. I do wonder how it is that so many Christians are so rich. When I think of all that money spent on big churches, houses, boats and cars, Ivy League college educations (and United States presidencies) for their children, and vacations to Europe, I have to wonder how much good it could be doing for the poor.

I am told that Jesus was talking just to that rich man, not all rich men. Of course, any rules that Christians want to follow, that are convenient and easy to abide by, are meant for everyone. Only those they don't particularly like are specific to persons long dead. I've also been told that Jesus didn't mean we couldn't be rich; he was just warning us about worshiping money above God. If only Jesus had said exactly that; but he didn't. He made it pretty clear to the rest of us that he meant for Christians to sell all they have and give the money to the poor. The poor are still waiting.

One of the strangest things that Jesus said is that people who believe in him and are saved will be able to drive out demons, speak new languages, pick up serpents, "and if they drink any deadly thing, it will not harm them. They will lay hands on the sick and they will recover." (Mark 16:17-18) There are some churches in which the believers handle snakes; some of them get bit and die. I guess they weren't true believers. I don't know of any Christian who can drink poison without being harmed—I don't even know any who will try. Most importantly, Christians lay hands on the sick all the time without healing them. If there are true Christians out there, they aren't giving us their signs.

The two greatest commandments, according to Jesus, are that you should love God with all your heart, mind and soul and you should love your neighbor as yourself. The way I see it, Biblical Christians only love the parts of God that are palatable to them and only follow his word where it suits them. They only seem to love neighbors who agree with them.

Who reads the Bible, anyway?

It would be helpful to me if all people who determined to call themselves Christians would read their own holy book. They should all be required to study, at the very least, the New Testament at length, not just the good parts, the quotable and palatable parts, but the whole of it.

I have had too many conversations in which I realized that the Christian I was speaking with knew less about his own Bible than I did. That is insupportable. If you're going to claim you believe in something, you ought to know full well what it is you are saying about yourself.

Most Christians go about their daily lives without considering their beliefs. They may sit in church on Sundays (though the majority forego church altogether) and hear snippets of the holy book that is supposed to be God's word—you'd think they'd want to memorize the entire thing—and then have satisfied themselves that they are indeed Christian.

I must say, I respect more the Biblical inerrantist who knows full well the ugliness of the Bible and calls it good than the Christian who claims the belief without having read the book at all. I have little doubt that if more Christians actually read the Bible, there would be fewer Christians.

Chapter Five

Religion Satisfies Certain Human Desires

A great deal of intelligence can be invested in ignorance when the need for illusion is deep.
—Saul Bellow, winner of the 1976 Nobel Prize in Literature

W hen I look at this world, when I see and experience no gods, demons, spirits, angels or any supernatural entities whatsoever, I think that the most likely answer to gods is that humans made them up. There are many unanswered questions regarding existence but, until some god makes itself known to all of us objectively, I have no reason to accept that it is there at all. The claim that a benevolent god exists and created me for a purpose is unbelievable to me.

So, why do people believe the unbelievable?

The fact that the Bible is loaded with supernatural imagery of things that no longer occur, if they ever did—animals that talk, magical fruit, God causing the Earth to swallow people up—does nothing to deter the person who wants to believe that the Bible is literally true and inspired by a god. Tertullian, one of the earliest apologists, wrote in his *Adversus Marcionem* the following bit of illogic: "And the Son of God died, which is immediately credible because it is absurd. And buried he rose again, which is certain because it is impossible." Only a strong desire to believe would cause a person to declare that the more incredible a claim is, the more likely it is to be true.

Why would otherwise intelligent people turn away from reason to devote part of their lives to what others see as a myth? Why do they see other stories of gods and miracles as myth...but claim their god and their miracles are true? There has to be something in it for them; and there is. The Christian theology fulfills certain basic, human desires. It offers people a sense of worth and specialness while at the same time reaffirming their feelings of self-loathing. It gives them a community in which they can feel understood and supported. It eases their fears about life and death, offers them hope for immortality. It also gives them a feeling of superiority, of having an edge over others.

We, as humans, have some basic desires. We want comfort and pleasure; we don't want lives filled with fear. There is nothing wrong with that and I don't mean to condemn Christianity or theism for fulfill-ing human needs. I'm not claiming there is or was some kind of conspiracy to do so in order to gain control over the masses. (While I do believe that people have used religion, Christianity in particular, to gain power, I don't think Christianity was specifically designed as a method of control.) I believe that fulfilling these needs is the role of religion. It's what we developed religion for.

In *The Dogma of Christ and Other Essays on Religion, Psychology and Culture* (Holt, Rinehart, & Winston, 1963), Erich Fromm explains the supportive nature of shared fantasies:

> The common fantasy satisfactions have an essential advan-tage over individual daydreams: by virtue of their universality, the fantasies are perceived by the conscious mind as if they were real. An illusion shared by everyone becomes a reality. The oldest of these collective fantasy satisfactions is re-ligion.

People believe in the supernatural, gods and Christianity so fer-vently, partly because such belief is reinforced in the community. When everyone else believes, it makes belief not merely acceptable, but preferable; more problematic, however, is that communal fantasy becomes a reality so ingrained in society that turning oneself from the illusion may be difficult, if not impossible, for the majority. Not all people succumb to the illusion. Many don't buy into it in the first place; others grow out of it; still others fall out of it only after a difficult period of transformation.

Michael Shermer, in his book *Why People Believe Weird Things: Pseudoscience, Superstition, and Other Confusions of Our Time* (WH Freeman, 1997), outlines twenty-five fallacies that lead to errors in thought and allow people to accept invalid ideas as truth. Among these fallacies are the belief that bold and forceful statements and the use of scientific language make a claim true; problems with placement of the burden proof; reasoning after the fact; rationalization of failures; and an inability to distinguish truth from false analogies, coincidence and appeals to ignorance. All the problems Shermer points out could be corrected among the majority if our education in critical thinking skills and science was improved.

As more and more people not only stop believing, but also make their nonbelief known, nonbelief, at least in the traditional salvation religions like Christianity, will become acceptable. Already we see a growing trend throughout the world toward more liberalized salvation religions as well as growing bases of ancient religions such as Wicca and paganism. Though traditional religions fulfill many people's needs; one needn't find a religion in order to have one's needs met.

The feeling of being special

Christianity tells humans that they were created special, by a god. Humans are the end result of God's yearning. He wanted a creature to worship and praise him. The Earth is merely the home he created for us. I haven't figured out what the rest of the universe is for yet but Earth was definitely created for human habitation and all the other animals were put here for man's pleasure and use. But, as some would say, due to Satan's interference or the fall of man, some things in the world are irritating to man, if not horrific...from cold germs and viruses to earthquakes and floods.

From an objective standpoint, the world appears to be under no supernatural influence. Good things and bad happen to believers and atheists alike. Still, feeling that you, either as an individual or as a species, were created special by an omnipotent, omni-benevolent (except for that Hell thing) god makes most of us feel good. It gives us the impression we are remarkable.

Christianity also explains the feelings that we all have from time to time that we are not so special. Most, if not all, humans suffer periodic bouts of self-loathing and the Christian theology explains this as our sinful nature. We are filled with lust, envy, greed, etc. because of our fall from grace. So humans are, at the same time, special to God and unworthy of his love and attention. It's a perfect psychological dichotomy, addressing both the need of worth and the explanation of self-loathing. It's quite an impressive theology, I'll admit, but merely addressing human nature insightfully is not enough to make the claim of deity true.

As an atheist, I don't feel that humans are special in any superior sense to other life on this planet. Certainly, we are the most intelligent species and the most creative, if not also the most adaptable (though I have to give roaches a good score on that final point). We are special in that way but, outside of that, I don't feel that humanity has a distinct place in the cosmos. We're just the highest rung on the ladder of intelligence at this point on this planet. When I think of the vastness of the universe, I imagine how comparably tiny we are.

Where do I turn to feel special? Humans can experience a sense of specialness in each individual's unique abilities and talents. We also are made to feel special by those we love and who love us. That is all the specialness I need.

A sense of meaning and purpose

Very much like the feeling of being special, is the sense of having some greater purpose, a feeling that one's life has a meaning beyond the few years we have here on Earth. I've been told by a few Christians that if there was no god, it would mean, for them, that this life had no meaning and purpose and they couldn't bear to live. I can understand that feeling, especially in view of the ugliness evident in our world. Many see life as a trial, as trudging from one problem to the next. They need to believe that there is a reason for the misery and pain of existence. I can appreciate that. It might make suffering easier if you believe that you will be greater blessed in an afterlife because of it. It may make it easier to endure if you sincerely believe there is a lesson to be learned from it, or that some good will come of it.

I don't believe there is a reason or purpose for life on Earth. I've met some Humanists, agnostics and atheists who believe that humans are here for a reason. They don't necessarily claim to know what that reason is, but they believe there is one just the same. I don't. I have no cause to believe there is a reason. I see no evidence of a reason or purpose to existence. I only know that I exist and I must make the most of it. That is my purpose.

Life is meaningless in the sense that one day I will not exist as I do now; and of course, the Sun will eventually burn out and all life on Earth will cease. Who thinks that far in advance? Who travels through life constantly at odds with the end of it, with the end of time? Atheists have the same kind of meaning in their lives as Christians. We, for some reason, don't have a need for any greater meaning than is apparent.

The feeling of security

Belief in a god allays fears of the unknown. It is a comforting thought that your spiritual father is there to take care of you and that death isn't really death. Death scares most people. I'm not sure why but it no doubt has a lot to do with instinct and survival. Death only scares me a little and only because I like living and want to keep doing it for a while longer. I realized, when I thought about it, that when I'm dead, I won't exist any longer and therefore, neither will any fear or sorrow that I associate with death. It won't matter once it's over. I think about the time before I was born. I didn't exist then and it didn't bother me. I imagine death will be little different. That gives me comfort.

Christians also take solace from knowing that their lives are guided and protected by their god. In reality, Christians are no more untouched by the horrors of living than the rest of us. They die in hurricanes and floods, they are murdered, they are killed in car crashes and plane crashes, drowned, burned to death, ravaged by disease just like the rest of us. Their god is not doing anything for them except giving them a pretense of protection through it all.

When they are saved, when they survive the flood, crash, attempted murder, etc., God or an angel was watching over them or their prayers were answered. When they don't survive, their loved ones agree it was God's will. If this gives them comfort, so be it. It wouldn't give me any. I am rather amused by the bumper stickers that proclaim "God is my co-pilot" as if this god will actually protect the driver from the horrors of this world. If that were true, if Christians never suffered the evils that other men did, it might be considered some evidence for the truth of their beliefs. Unfortunately, belief in God makes little difference in when and in what manner death finds you. If I knew that a god was watching over me while a man with a knife attacked me, stabbing me to death, I'd hardly consider myself blessed for his lack of attention just because he considered it my time to go or because he decided that I should die in such a terrifying way, or worse, because he won't interfere with the free will he gave the murderer. I find no comfort in that idea. I'd rather more likely feel as if I were entertainment, in the manner of Job, perhaps.

I do, however, take great comfort in many things about this life, as unpleasant as it may seem at times. I'm consoled in knowing that many of us are striving to love one another and to make peace. Some of us are lunatics and go about murdering others or abusing children, it is true. Some of us are really filled with hate. But I can look past those few (and yes, considering how many of us there are on this planet, they are few) to the majority of us who, I believe, want to be kind and loving and peaceful.

I take comfort in knowing that this life is temporary and that each day of it counts greatly. I take comfort in that because it is my excuse, if you will, to take time out to read, write, play with my children, watch television and movies, to enjoy this precious time I have. I have little doubt that many Christians treat life in the same manner.

I take comfort in knowing that the stuff I am made of has existed since the beginning of time as we know it. The stuff of the universe is not only all around us—we are it. The same particles of matter in me, that are me, will exist forever, as far as I can tell. In a sense, what I am made of is immortal. No, I don't believe that I, myself, my mind, will exist beyond my lifetime. While I do take comfort in the hope that my progeny will continue for as long as humans do, I realize that the only constant is change and that at some point, humanity will evolve so far beyond its present state that I will be too insignificant to count as ancestor, or it will die out. But that won't matter because that substance that is me, is the stuff of the universe and will go on. Not that I'll notice...I'll be dead.

A sense of community

Religion also gives people an important sense of community. Having a church social outlet must be very helpful to the human animal. I appreciate people's attachments to their church families, if they get a sense of support and community from them. I can imagine that would be difficult to let go of once you are a part of it. Of course, I also imagine that there are some people who become part of a church social group for reasons other than genuine belief and sincere social intercourse. I'm thinking of savvy business people who might join the wealthiest and largest churches in town for contacts.

Nonetheless, it can't be argued that the human animal is not social and doesn't need social outlets. When I first realized atheism, I felt as if I were alone in the world. Luckily, the Internet has changed the social landscape, allowing nonbelievers to find each other more easily and congregate in our own way.

A sense of superiority

I don't know what it is about humans, not being a social psychologist myself, but they generally seem to have a need to feel superior to others. Throughout human history we can witness humans trying to prove their superiority through their gods, wars, racism, sexism and any other method they could find. Mankind is a fearful species—fearful of death; fearful of the unknown; fearful of change—and fearful of people who are different from themselves. Humans try to conquer that fear by demolishing those who are different in order to prove that their own way is the right way.

Religions, especially the traditional faiths like Christianity, do this for a lot of people, most especially fundamentalists. The fundamentalist knows he's right. He's got the right deity, the right religion, the right church, and the right interpretation of his holy book. He is saved and the next guy probably isn't. Definitely those Catholics aren't saved—unless you ask them. For sure those Jehovah's Witnesses aren't—unless you ask them. We know the Mormons are lost souls—unless you ask one of them. But this guy, the fundamentalist Christian, he is definitely one of the elect. When the rapture comes, he'll be gone and all you'll find left of him are his clothes...if you believe the movie.

The point is people like that have to feel that they are better than somebody, preferably a lot of somebodies. The smaller the group of chosen, the more powerful and special they feel. There is a word for that: elitism. The elitist Christian doesn't have to be a fundamentalist; but a fundamentalist is always an elitist.

While I can agree that the experience of being right is a good one, I haven't found satisfaction in a feeling of superiority over others. It more often than not causes me to feel sad. It's not something I practice. If I am smarter than one person on a certain subject, I keep in mind that there are others who are smarter than I.

I think that many Christians feel the same way however there are those who feel superiority over others not because of anything they know or can do, but simply because they believe they have found a truth that others have not. Unfortunately, I have met some that continue in their superior attitude while seeming to temper it with an expression of pity for the unsaved. This type of person is always sweet, almost apologetic, about being one of the elect and claims to be truly sorrowful for the fate of the lost souls, knowing what they will endure in their eternal torment. It saddens them deeply and gives them a good excuse to try to save them. This attitude may convince the Christian that he isn't elitist, because he expresses pity instead of scorn, but his mannerisms betray him.

I don't think anything can be done to end the elitism of Christianity as long as the concepts of Hell and salvation are a part of it. If mankind needs to be saved and the only way to do it is through their god Jesus, there is nothing but elitism in the cards. They can't escape it. Only a Universalist Christian can.

Some atheists may consider their intellect a source of superiority; but honestly, a person doesn't have to be an atheist to be an intellectual. And of course, not all atheists are intellectuals, or even very smart.

I don't have a comparable feeling of elitism. I don't feel that I belong to a special group or am better than any group of people.

Power

The person in the pew can have a feeling of power via his elitism, no matter how subtle, and, for the American Christian, through the knowledge that he is part of the majority. The people on the altars and those that make up the church hierarchy have a different kind of power. Power, influence and control are major motivators for many people in the business of god.

I have no equivalent feeling with atheism. Atheists, as far as I can tell, have no political power. I think a lot of Christians would disagree. For many, the attempts to maintain a secular public school system and a secular government are driven by an atheist or Humanist conspiracy to force people to give up their religion. To me, these are simply the results of adhering to the idea of separation of church and state. The secularist has no desire to keep people from worshiping a god. That is a personal choice we all may make. The secularist simply wants to protect the minority from the majority.

Not all people in this country believe a god exists. It is wrong for the majority to force the minority to act as if it believes in a god when it doesn't. The phrase "In God We Trust" should not be on our money, or displayed in government buildings. The phrase "...under God" should not have been allowed to be inserted into our Pledge of Allegiance in 1954 during the shameful McCarthy era. The Ten Commandments are distinctly religious and do not belong on monuments in judicial buildings.

It's frustrating to hear people say that the majority should be allowed to place its religious view into our government and force others to claim a god exists when pledging loyalty to their country. We are the majority, they say, and atheists should just ignore it, go along with it, or worse, leave the country if they don't like it. It's so easy to overlook oppression when you are in the majority. Atheists are just as much citizens of this country as theists. We should not be put into positions in which we have to ignore or tolerate god belief in our government. Theists claim we are trying to force them to hide their worship, but that is not true. They are free to build churches and congregate within them. They are free to utter prayers at any time they wish, as long as they are not forcing other people to do so as well. Freedom and justice *for all* is not possible if this is "one nation, under God."

Christians claim that atheists made praying in school illegal; they say we took God out of school, but that is not true. Students and faculty can utter silent prayers at any time they wish. What is not legal (nor moral) is a person standing before a class or assembly and calling for prayer. Why is that so difficult to understand? Why is it considered such a restriction? Why must Christians insist on praying publicly and calling others to pray with them, knowing full well that such an audience may consist of non-Christians?

Non-Christian students can opt out, they say. But why should non-Christians and atheists feel forced to leave a classroom or assembly just so Christians can pray? Christians can pray in church, at home, and silently to themselves at any time. Why must they insist on everyone joining them? Why must those who do not wish to, be singled out?

I think the crux of the matter is that Christians believe that anyone who doesn't believe the way they do is not only wrong, but
immoral, and therefore, tolerance of their position is out of the
question. There is a movement in the United States toward a theo-
cratic government. It is insidious, sly, but becoming more and more
apparent. I am awed by the technique the religious right has em-
ployed, infiltrating government positions, altering their language so
as to appear less fanatical than they actually are. They are doing a
great job; most people are being lulled into believing they are
harmless; most people don't bother to research before they vote;
most people don't care.

This leads to the kind of power and control I'm talking about, akin
to the Taliban in Afghanistan. There are Christians in the United States
who would like to establish a theocracy here. They want political
power so that they can instill their version of morality, of god, and of
government on all the people. That is very frightening to an atheist, as
it most likely is also to a pagan or Wiccan or any other non-traditional
believer. Fighting against such power and control is the cause of lib-
erty, rather than another form of control. It is the opposite: it's standing
up for the minority, so they aren't trampled by a self-righteous, elitist
majority.

A sense of justice

The world is a frightening and dangerous place for some people. There
is evil everywhere and the bad people don't always get their just deserts. People are getting away with murder. People are bilking others
out of their hard-earned savings and walking away free. People are
causing pain and torment in others' lives and never face prosecution.
People break promises, seduce young girls, divorce their wives, cheat
on their husbands, betray their friends and are never punished. If you
are a victim of any sort of violence, betrayal or discrimination, it can be
upsetting to know that the person or group of people who hurt you continues to live their lives as if they've done nothing wrong; some even
prosper. Christianity, in particular, provides a nice sense of justice. You
can believe that, even though your enemies aren't punished here on
Earth, in the afterlife, they will be.

There is some justice. We have laws, and courts to deal with those
who break them. We have some laws governing treatment of people but

not all injuries are covered by law. There are many instances when you are hurt and nothing can be done about it. It may appear that there is no justice.

Part of justice is in your attitude. What will you make of the events in your life? What will you learn from them, how will you handle them and how will you treat the person who hurt you? Your attitude affects your outlook—it is your outlook. People who can forgive more easily are happier; people who hold grudges are miserable. I can appreciate wanting to know that there is some ultimate justice that will balance everything at some point...but I have to wonder how much is the desire truly for justice, and how much is it for revenge?

Immortality

The desire for immortality is, perhaps, the strongest desire among humans. Most of us are terrified of death. Religion promises immortality. You can't get any more comforting than that. You won't die. You will live on perhaps in a different form. Better yet, all those people who believe exactly like you do (so you don't have to hate or fear them) will join you in a paradise and all those people who didn't believe what you believed (so you hated and feared them) or the ones who did very bad things to you will suffer an eternal torment in Hell. You can't get any more elitist than that.

I don't want immortality. The desire for eternity and the promise of it given by religions throughout time is evidence that gods and religion are man made. We need comfort, we need justice, we need to suppress our fear of death, so we eagerly believe whatever would satisfy our needs; and we teach this salve to our children and to anyone else who will listen. I suppose I can understand this fear, and the hope that religion offers. But I don't want it; I don't want a comforting lie. I don't want comfort for comfort's sake. I am much more concerned with honesty, truthfulness, and what is real.

What Do I Desire?

As a rationalist, I desire truth above all else. I do not want to be swayed by my fears, my feelings of self-righteousness, or my emotions. I want the truth. Even if it's depressing, discomforting, or ugly, I prefer the truth.

I don't fault any person for believing in comforting ideas but, once those ideas become dogma, once the claim of superiority or the threat of punishment is made, once the attempt is made to control my life and force me to accept a particular religion as reality, I will stand against it. I have no choice. If others are to be truly free to believe, I must be free to not believe.

Chapter Six

The Differences between Us

People like to think that most others are just like they are; it validates them. Some people are worse about it than others. I've known people to insist I would behave exactly as they had if I'd been in their situation, no matter how I might deny that I would. People have a hard time understanding that, while we are all human and pretty much wired the same, we do differ, in some cases extraordinarily. Difficult as it may seem to theists, I truly do not believe in deity and find no evidence for the existence of such. It may be hard for some to accept because they think that I am very much like them and experience the same things in the same way they do, think the same, and am persuaded by the same things they are. Because they might think that, they have to believe that what keeps me from accepting that god is obvious, must be some sort of unwillingness or blindness on my part.

The differences that separate theists from atheists lie on a scale, something like a number line. At one end is rationalism and at the other is emotionalism. Rational does not mean smart and emotional stupid. Rational doesn't mean sane while emotional means insane.

Rationalism is a philosophy whose adherents rely on reason to determine reality. Certainly, we are humans and can't entirely separate ourselves from intuition and emotion. The extreme end of rationalism is impossible, as well as unattractive. At the other end, emotionalism in the extreme is insanity. All sane humans utilize their reason to some extent. Most humans, in my estimation (a nonscientific one, I grant you) lie just to the right of center, leaning more toward emotionalism than rationalism. They allow their feelings, hopes, aspirations and intuition to guide them. They want reality to be a certain way and are willing to accept or deny evidence to bolster that view. They may also feel that science can't explain everything and that it is quite possible for another realm to exist which can't be studied objectively so we must rely on our senses and "spirit" to explore it.

Some people, most notably the majority of scientists, are on the left, more rational in their approach to reality. They rely less on their emotions to guide them in the pursuit of truth. The farther toward rationalism a person is, the more likely he is to think that what we can know, we only know through objective study. All else—revelation, authoritarian discourse, hope and subjective experience—yields untestable, unprovable results and therefore can not be relied upon to offer us any truth.

I am a rationalist. There is no objective evidence for a realm beyond the reality we know to exist and I refuse to create a belief about any such place. I do not trust the subjective experiences of others as necessarily truthful; nor do I consider ancient, unverifiable texts a valuable tool in the search for truth. Rationalism may well be called my world view. I view the world as the reality that can be objectively experienced. Any other phenomena, being that it emanates from either my own subjective experience or is related to me by someone else who claims to have had the subjective experience, is without objective reality. It can't be demonstrated, reproduced, tested, evaluated or measured; therefore, it can't be said to factually exist.

I suppose one could accept that it *might* exist. Anything might exist. Unicorns might. Garblesnooks on a planet billions of miles from here might and, yes, gods might exist. But they do not interact with the world and humans in an objective, measurable way so their existence can't be verified. You wouldn't believe in the garblesnooks, if I asked you to, would you? It doesn't really matter to you one way or another if they do or don't exist so you lose nothing by ignoring my insane belief. And you recognize that I am insane when I claim they exist and communicate with me.

Yet, millions of people accept that various versions of a god exist, that at least one of these actually made himself into one of us and had himself killed for our salvation only to rise again from the dead. Millions of people believe this unverifiable, untestable, unprovable story and claim it is perfectly sane to do so, perfectly rational even. Why? Because their world view is opposite mine.

Millions of people are either brought up with, or accept at a later age, the idea that a supernatural realm exists. Of those who are brought up with the idea, it is easy to understand the strength with which they hold to that view. For those who weren't instilled with the idea as children, society offers them plenty of reason as young people and adults to accept the world view, mostly in the form of community support and acceptance—everyone else believes, and they really want you to believe too.

Humans, not to be too hard on them, are rather stupid creatures. Look at the things some of us believe. Some believe that the stars and planets and their alignment at the time of our births will determine our personalities and even the events of our lives. Biblical Christians believe astrology is witchcraft and a sin. Some believe that aliens from other worlds visit the Earth regularly and often take humans aboard their spaceships and perform experiments on them. I can't begin to imagine the Biblical Christian view on that, but no doubt it has something to do with Satan. How many millions of people call psychic hotlines and pay untold sums of money to hear someone finagle information from them and feed it back to them calling it ESP? People believe ridiculous things for two reasons: they lack solid critical thinking skills, leaving them gullible, and they have already accepted that there is another realm beyond the objective reality of the world.

Once the idea of supernaturalism is accepted, any number of beliefs can be had regarding it. There are all sorts of religious beliefs in the world. In the United States alone you'll find paganism, Voodoo, Wicca and Native American spiritualism, just to name a few. There are millions of people who don't subscribe to any particular dogma but simply believe whatever strikes their fancy: reincarnation, karma, chakras, or auras. Once you've accepted a hidden, subjectively experienced realm, anything goes.

For the dogmatists in the U.S., who tend to be rather controlling people, the most popular belief is, of course, Christianity. Its story is no more believable than is astrology's or astral projection's, but it is more acceptable because it is the more popular belief. Popularity doesn't equal truth by any means. For how many hundreds of years did European culture claim that the Sun revolved around the Earth?

It wasn't true and the attitude that led to our realization that it was a lie was skepticism. Someone had to doubt the popular belief and dare to check it out.

The supernaturalist and rationalist world views are opposite and there is no middle ground between them. Once a person finds himself on one side or the other he can not reconcile the two. The problem is not that the rationalist hasn't experienced what the supernaturalist has; he simply doesn't interpret the experience in the same manner and doesn't give as much weight to his feelings in the matter. We have the same sensations, emotions, fears and desires but what a theist may claim as a holy spirit within him, may be to the atheist no more than great joy.

I do not believe that there is anything a theist can say to a rationalist to convince him that a supernatural realm exists. Some might claim this is close-minded, but I don't agree. I am open to the possibility but I am not so open as to accept *any* notion. I'm certainly not going to accept something just because someone tells me it's true. That's called skepticism and there's not a thing wrong with it. We should all be skeptical. You can't just tell me there's a supernatural realm; you have to give me evidence. Unfortunately, the evidence I've been given thus far is woefully inadequate. I'm told, "You won't accept my evidence because you just don't want to believe." Well, that is somewhat correct. I can't believe something that I don't think is true and I certainly don't want to attempt to delude myself or pretend. Any notion that has to be *believed in* is obviously lacking material evidence. Believing in things is not rational.

Evidence for God

For hundreds of years now, atheists have raised objections to belief in the existence of god. Christians have responded with answers to those objections. It's a "yes, but..." sort of conversation we've had going for so long that, when looking at it from the perspective of the long haul, it looks as if believers and atheists are just talking past each other. It doesn't matter what the atheist says, the Christian has an answer for it. The explanation is enough for the Christian to maintain his belief but not enough to convince the atheist of the existence of a god.

What I offer here is not my own objection to belief in god. Theists believe that a god exists and nothing I say is going to change their minds. Instead, I'd like to outline the arguments I have heard on both sides, briefly, to make known the positions of most atheists and Christian apologists on the issues.

As far as I'm concerned, it's a draw. All the evidence has been laid out on the table. The rationalist atheist accepts this evidence as all that Christianity has to offer and finds it unconvincing. The believer accepts it as proof. That's all there is to the problem and all there ever will be. Atheists and believers are divided over one crucial difference: our opinions differ greatly on what constitutes evidence.

✕✕✕✕

The only real objection to the existence of God on the atheist side is lack of evidence. There is no evidence that a god exists. The theist's response to this objection is that there is ample evidence for God's existence. The evidence is as follows:

✓ You can't get something from nothing
✓ Life exists
✓ Miracles
✓ The Bible and prophecy
✓ Answered prayer
✓ Subjective experience
✓ The effects of belief
✓ The spread of Christianity

I will briefly explain why none of these constitutes evidence for a rationalist.

You can't get something from nothing

Theists say that nothing comes from nothing so something had to exist before the universe existed. They say that everything has a cause so there must be a First Cause. This is known as the Cosmological Argument for the existence of God. It may be an argument, but it's not evidence for a god. We haven't established as fact that everything must have a cause, and if everything does need a cause, God would also need one. If God could have existed forever, why couldn't the universe, or something else that led to it? You can't just slap God at the beginning and give it special status and expect the rationalist to go along. We don't know what, if anything, existed before the universe came about.

People much smarter than you and I are studying it right now. I don't know how the universe came to be, what existed before it, if it's eternal, or if there was a god that created it and neither do you. We don't know. That isn't evidence for God. It's only evidence of our limited knowledge.

Life exists

As we've seen, evidence for God usually begins with statements of incredulity. The believer says things like, "All this could not have happened just by chance. The odds are astronomical that mankind would emerge from lower forms of existence." The problem with these remarks is that, because you don't know how something came to be doesn't leave you to invent an answer with the expectation that the rest of us must accept it as correct.

Theists say that because life exists against insurmountable odds, there must be a supernatural force behind the universe; but the fact that something exists is not proof of anything except that something exists. It has nothing to do with whether or not a god or gods exist. There is no reason to apply a god concept to everything that we don't understand or that seems highly unlikely to us.

Theistic claims regarding odds are misleading. They assume mankind was the necessary result, that there was a process at work that had to result in humans and they assume astronomical odds after the fact, which is nonsense. The universe exists; mankind exists. The die is cast—the odds are one. Odds are expressed as numbers between zero and one. Something that is absolutely certain not to occur has odds of zero. An outcome that is absolutely certain to occur has odds of one. Once an event has occurred, the odds for its occurrence are one.

Take a deck of cards, for example. Let's say I ask you to lay all the cards out in a line across the room. When you lay them out they will be in a particular order. After you lay them out do you marvel at the odds against them being in that order? Do you claim the odds against them being in that order are so against that supernatural powers must have been at work? No, you simply laid them out in that order...they had to be in *some* order, right? The odds of them being in that order are one, because you are calculating the odds after the fact.

Let's suppose I list all the cards in the deck in any order I wish beforehand and then ask you to calculate the odds of you laying them all out in exactly that order after shuffling to your heart's content. The odds are highly against your doing so but you notice that we've decided what the outcome will be before we've laid out the cards. Calculating the odds that life would arise on Earth is like going back in time and predicting that life (or humans specifically) would arise exactly as it already has and then claiming the odds are so ridiculously high that a god must exist. It's meaningless and nonsensical to do this.

Theists also claim extraordinary odds against creatures like us simply popping into existence. Life couldn't arise from non-life, they say, as if life came to exist fully formed, something like a tornado blowing through a junkyard resulting in a 747. Cells don't just pop into being. No one (but theists) has made the claim that cells, much less entire complex organisms such as humans, simply appeared. When you break the process down into tiny steps, one after another, each building on and adding to the former, the odds aren't so great anymore, nor the idea so incredible. But many theists have some sort of mental block in this regard.

Creationists ask how the eye could have possibly evolved as the complex, interwoven series of parts that it is, when the individual parts can't work without each other. What good is half an eye? They're not thinking in steps—small alterations, little by little over millions of years, each step adding to the one before it and allowing the organism in question to survive better than those that didn't get that tiny improvement.

One light-sensitive cell is better than none. Half an eye is more beneficial than no eye. Each step, each little mutation that benefited the organism helped it to survive and reproduce. It's not odds that are the problem; it's letting incredulity, ignorance and wishful thinking clog one's ability to grasp the real scientific explanation, rather than simply accepting without question the nonscientific attempts to refute it.

Creationists seem to think they can prove God by disproving evolution. They are stuck with a false dichotomy: we either evolved naturally, or the god of the Bible exists. There are plenty of other possibilities but because their real enemy is scientific intellectualism, they realize they must try to make evolutionary theories look as bad as possible. They do a good job of muddying the waters, confusing people with a lot of scientific-sounding jargon, lying, misquoting and misrepresenting people and facts.

Species adapt among their own kind, they agree. The peppered moths certainly changed color with the tree bark over in England. Yes, we can watch the changes in bacteria in the laboratory. But one species will never change into another. Fish don't turn into amphibians. Reptiles don't turn into birds. If they had, you'd find missing links in the fossil record. Where are the fossils of half-bird, half-reptile creatures? They say you can't find them because speciation is a lie.

Creationists do not think small enough. Species don't "turn into" others; they gradually change, step by step over millions of years, until what you have doesn't look at all like what you started with. Who decides what a reptile is, anyway? Who says when a creature is an amphibian or a reptile? What is a platypus? Humans make these distinctions. Humans put life forms into groups. Plenty of animals are in between or don't fit well into one group. There are fish that can breathe oxygen for short periods of time; they use their fins to scoot from puddle to puddle; can't you imagine that after a few million more years they'll be able to breathe air all the time and their fins will have changed to something more like legs? Any changes in that species that make moving from puddle to puddle easier will enable it to survive and reproduce to make better mudskippers until finally, you've got something that's not a fish anymore.

Each and every fossil we find is another link between species. Each fossil is a transitional form. It's all transitional, constantly changing. There is no missing link.

When theists point to complex occurrences such as the human eye as proof of God, they are proffering a theory called Intelligent Design. ID Theory is the new Creationism. Pushing Creationism hasn't worked because intelligent people have trouble accepting the stories of creation in the Bible as true, when they blatantly contradict reality. Day and night could not have existed before the Sun, for instance; neither could vegetation have survived. And yet, according to the Bible, the perfect, inerrant word of the almighty god of the universe, day and night have nothing to do with the Sun, and plants don't utilize photosynthesis. We know that the sky is not solid and doesn't separate us from water. Rain isn't the "floodgates of the sky" being opened. We are sure humans are not made of dust, men have the same number of ribs as women, that serpents don't talk and magic trees bearing corrupting fruit don't exist except in mythology.

So the movement stepped back and tried a new tactic: Intelligent Design. There is no mention of the Bible in ID theory; the god at the back of it is not identified. ID theory is all about science, or rather, pseudoscience. Complexity and design in nature are highlighted to explain that design implies a designer. When you find a watch on the ground, so the story goes, you reason that it had a designer. When you look at the human eye or the (seemingly) impossible flight capability of the bumblebee, you reason, as well, that such could not have been brought into existence (wholesale, they mean but never say) or made possible without a superior, intelligent force to direct it.

ID theorists like to talk about the Second Law of Thermodynamics. This law, they say, proves that evolution is impossible. If the universe is moving from order to chaos, how could complex life-forms have possibly arisen out of slime? I'm no scientist, mind you, but if the average person took just a small amount of time to read up on the basics they, like me, could immediately recognize the failure of this argument. The only people who make the assertion are those who neither understand evolutionary theory, nor the Second Law of Thermodynamics. The law relates to entropy in closed systems. The Earth is not a closed system; it receives energy from the Sun. If the Earth was subject to the Second Law, there would be no life here at all. Of course, Creationists would simply invoke the supernatural powers of God to explain that.

Once the credulous agree on the points raised by Intelligent Design theorists, the claim is made for the Christian god, and because we live in a Christian-dominated society where everyone believes in and prays to this imagined creature, another soul is saved.

Intelligent Design is Creationism in disguise. No one is fooling the skeptics. Complexity is understandable if you stop thinking of it as arising complete in one fell swoop. If you learn to think in billions upon billions of years, thousands upon thousands of generations, one tiny change after another each building on and improving the survivability of an organism over those millennia, speciation isn't an impossible concept to embrace.

Abiogenesis is the next logical point of contention. Even if you can convince a Biblical literalist that theories of evolution best explain the fossil evidence, they will still claim the odds of life arising from non-life are astronomical. This is another argument from incredulity; they can't imagine it, so it couldn't be true.

Have you heard of the chimps with the typewriters? If an infinite number of chimpanzees sat typing, what are the odds that one of them would eventually type the Declaration of Independence? Pretty high? Not really. With an infinite number, and an eternity, eventually they would type out all possible letter sequences. But the Creationist isn't thinking this way. He's thinking: put a few monkeys in a room with typewriters and then what are the odds? Because the Creationist thinks in big steps, he's imagining the wholesale, one-time chance of a chimp clacking away on the keyboard and producing the Declaration complete.

That's not a proper model of abiogenesis. Chemicals didn't have to start from the beginning each time with nothing, attempting bonds over and over from scratch, until by some wild chance they formed into a bacteria. No one claims it happened with just one trial, done over and over again. Instead, billions of the available chemicals interacted over billions of years, producing combinations until some of those combinations led to what we call a life form.

Think of the chimps again. This time, imagine just one chimp at a keyboard and let's say that "life" equals the phrase "When in the course of human events." Only combinations that match the phrase "work." Combinations that don't match are discarded because they don't "fit." The first round might match a few letters. Those letters aren't discarded; the chimp doesn't have to start all over again with a blank sheet. Those matches "work;" they "fit." They are advantageous because they link together; they form building blocks to which the next try can add. In the next round, more hits are produced that match the building blocks linked together so far. It won't take very many rounds before the chimp will succeed in typing out the phrase that we've decided equals "life."

Remember that we are the designators of labels. We choose what we will call life and what we call non-life. We know that ancient Earth contained the necessary chemicals; we know that these chemicals bond; and we know that the earliest form of life was extremely elementary, nothing more than simple molecules.

It's that problem of not thinking small again. Creationists think big. Things pop into existence fully formed in their world view. They imagine simple chemicals lumping together to form bacteria and marvel at the odds against it. They can't seem to imagine tiny building blocks linking to each other, adding more blocks, and more, until something exists that is no longer merely a chemical compound, but living matter. Then after more steps, over more time, something like bacteria evolved.

There are plenty of other problems with Creationist attacks on theories of evolution and abiogenesis. You can read about them on the Talk Origins website at *www.talkorigins.org*.

Miracles

Christians point to miracles as evidence of God's existence but most of the miracles they point to are in the Bible. We can't use the Bible miracles as evidence of God because they are in the very book which God is claimed to have inspired. The Bible is not evidence because it's nothing more than a very old, inaccurate book until it is proven otherwise. The Bible is fiction until it can be shown to be factual.

Theists also point to modern-day miracles as evidence but none have been shown to be anything more than mass hysteria, wishful thinking or, at worst, fraud. Crying statues of Mary or Jesus' face baked into muffins have never been shown to be the work of any supernatural entity. Jesus' face on the side of a building isn't a miracle; it's humans finding patterns in their environment. That's what humans do.

Have you ever noticed that only Catholics get Mary in their miracles? If you are going to claim miracles are evidence for God, then shouldn't you be Catholic? How can a person discount Mary miracles but accept gold fillings showing up in teeth at mass prayer-fests as evidence? Don't you think that Muslims have their miracle stories too? Is that evidence that Allah is the one true god and Mohammed is his prophet? Shouldn't everyone convert to Islam then?

Miraculous healings are reported but they are never documented by the medical profession, are never written up in medical journals and never involve obviously impossible events like lost limbs suddenly reappearing, people losing their heads and then growing them back, or people coming back from the dead after embalming and burial. No, they're always unverifiable healings, like tumors disappearing, bones growing a few centimeters, legs lengthening, eye-sight improving. After the healings take place, there's no follow up; nobody checks to see if the lady had a tumor in the first place, nor if it's gone. Nobody checks to see if the person puts her glasses back on later. If God exists and performs miracles, why aren't they better ones?

Miracle stories are almost always given to atheists second-hand. When asked for evidence of God's existence, the theist may say his best friend's cousin, or his friend's grandmother, or a group of kids he goes to school with had an experience. There's never any documentation and rarely any first-hand testimony.

I did hear first-hand testimony once. The miracle involved God, or a good spirit, fighting with Satan, or an evil spirit, for control of a radio. My correspondent was a young man whose family had been in turmoil for some time. His mother was sure that she was possessed by a demon and that evil spirits were trying to take control of the family. They set their radio station to gospel music in an attempt to ward off the demons. The young man claimed that he witnessed the radio dial move, changing the station from gospel to something else. He believed that the evil spirits were changing the station. The dial moved, he was sure, because he saw it with his own eyes. Looking beyond the paltry nature of the miracle, it doesn't surprise me at all that this young man believed that he saw the radio dial move. His family obviously believed bizarre things and was in a high state of anxiety at the time. But I don't believe that the station changed, or that he saw the dial move. I believe he imagined the entire thing, possibly even in hindsight.

I have been asked what it would take to convince me a miracle had taken place. It's very simple, really. If people's severed limbs suddenly reappeared, and we had documented proof of it (including the remains of the severed limb), I'd be pretty convinced. If dead and embalmed bodies came back to life, and we had the medical documentation to prove it, that would convince me. If Christians really could ask anything in Jesus' name and get it, they would have some good evidence for Christ. If they really could handle venomous snakes and drink poison without being hurt, I'd think there was something there. If they really could just lay their hands on the sick and heal them, I'd start considering it. But they can't. Faith healers are frauds. There have been no documented miraculous healings; they are always obscure, unverifiable events. Nobody ever shows documented evidence. Let's see Benny Hinn make a severed leg reappear! That would be a miracle. But it never happens and it never will.

If there was a flood and only Christians survived it because the flood waters miraculously flowed around their homes, or better yet, over them leaving them in pockets of air space, then I'd be with you, thinking maybe there's something to this God thing. If Christians, or those who believe in the right god, anyway, always walked away from fiery plane crashes without a scratch on them, then I'd begin to wonder. All the above goes for Islam and Muslims or Judaism and Jews or any other god belief that says miracles prove it.

But things like that don't happen. There are no miracles. There are only humans believing in miracles. That's not evidence of anything except the human imagination and the power of belief.

The Bible and prophecy

Many Christians claim that God exists because the prophecies in the Bible came true. But, believers only point out prophecies that were apparently fulfilled and either have no knowledge of or conveniently forget to mention all the prophecies that went unfulfilled. Any objective study of Biblical prophecy will uncover a sad history of failure. Some of the prophecies did apparently come true, but not all. The ones that did are suspect because the stories of them coming true are told about in the same book in which the prediction is made. We can't trust them. Just look at the New Testament stories about the actions of Jesus done for the express purpose of fulfilling supposed prophecy. Well, sure, if you get the book of prophecy out and start fulfilling...that's cheating.

Obviously the authors of the New Testament were familiar with the Old. Why should we assume the authors of the books of the Old Testament were not aware of books written before their own? They may have rewritten the older books to make it seem as if a prophecy had occurred. How do you know the books weren't written at the same time and some only made to seem as if some were written earlier and predicted events that the author witnessed himself? How do you know that the author didn't just write that a prophecy was fulfilled whether it was or not? There is also a chance that when you predict one hundred events, some of them may happen, so the fact that some of the prophecies were fulfilled means nothing beyond chance in action (if the stories are true to begin with).

Many of the verses that are claimed to be prophecies don't read like prophecy at all. A prophecy is an inspired revelation of divine will, a description of what the inspiring deity has planned for its people. Prophecy is prediction, inspired by a god. Much of what passes as prophecy simply isn't. If a prophet in the Bible makes a prediction, it is supposed to be inspired of God. If he turns out to have been wrong, he was a false prophet.

Ezekiel, in Chapter 13, receives God's feelings regarding false prophets:

> Their visions are false and their divinations a lie. They say, "the Lord declares," when the Lord has not sent them; yet they expect their words to be fulfilled. Have you not seen false visions and uttered lying divinations when you say, "The Lord

declares," though I have not spoken? Therefore, this is what the
Sovereign Lord says: Because of your false words and lying vi-
sions, I am against you... (Ezekiel 13:6-8)

If God inspired a prophet to make a prediction, we must assume
that it would happen in the way the prediction is made. If God inspires
the prophet, he can't be wrong. We can assume, then, that any prophet
who predicted something and turned out to be wrong was a false
prophet and God was against him.

Apologists like to pick out some predictions that worked, and then
claim that all the prophecy in the Bible was accurate. They tend to
leave out any verses that are inaccurate. Take Ezekiel, himself. The
claim is made that Ezekiel predicted that Egypt would "never again
exalt itself above other nations. I [God] will make it so weak that it
will never again rule over the other nations." (Ezekiel 29:15) But the
prophet also said that God would make Egypt a ruin and a desolate
wasteland for forty years, that no man or animal would pass
through it during that time. That never happened. Those other verses
are conveniently glossed over as merely a prediction that Egypt would
be ruined but would recover. But it reads just like the rest of the
prophecy, distinct, clear and specific—and it was false. Ezekiel's
prophecy also includes a dispersal of the Egyptian people and the dry-
ing up of the Nile, neither of which happened. But the apologists
won't tell you about those. That is the pattern of prophecy in the Bible. Only those few verses that appear to have been correctly
predicted are offered as proof of the truth of the book. All the others
are left out.

Where are the prophecies of modern day occurrences in the Bible?
Some televangelists illustrate them with charts on their walls explaining
all the figurative language in the Bible and how it predicted what is
happening today; but it's all shadow play. You can interpret those supposed prophecies to mean anything you want them to mean. We have
proof of this when we study the history of modern-day prophetic interpretation, when we learn how numerous preachers convinced their
flocks the end was near and nothing happened; they'd go back to the
book and reinterpret everything. Next year, they'd say. I suppose it is
best that real facts are usually left out of prophecies; it makes them
harder to show inaccurate for those persons unfamiliar with the previ-
ous generations' interpretations.

Those verses that Christians claim predict the coming of Christ don't look at all like prophecy. It's as if early apologists searched through the Bible looking for anything that might remotely be construed as telling of the coming of Jesus and slapped the prophecy label all over it. That, to me, is disingenuous; but it has been a tactic of the Christian community from the beginning to create evidence where none exists.

Isaiah 53, for instance, sounds eerily similar to the trials of Jesus.

> Yet it was our infirmities that he bore, our sufferings that he endured...but he was pierced for our offenses, crushed for our sins...but the Lord laid upon him the guilt of us all...the will of the Lord shall be accomplished through him.

Unfortunately, the scripture in question doesn't read like a prophecy—a prediction; it's written in past tense and is describing the nation of Israel, not one man. I have to wonder if some verses in the Old Testament weren't simply hinted at in the stories of Jesus to give them more credence.

Isaiah 7:14 says, "Therefore the Lord himself will give you this sign: the virgin shall be with child, and bear a son, and shall name him Immanuel." Unfortunately, this prophecy is fulfilled later in the same book. In Chapter 8:3-4, the prophetess "conceived and bore a son." There are other problems with this prophecy. The word *almah* is translated elsewhere in the Old Testament as maiden, not virgin. There is another word for virgin, *bethulah*; but it seems many translators preferred to make the maiden a definite virgin in this verse. And, of course, Jesus' mother never referred to her son as Immanuel.

Whenever you attempt to show a contradiction or error in the Bible, you're likely to be told that you've taken the verse out of context. Yet, every so-called prediction of Jesus in the Old Testament is gotten by taking the verses out of context. Nowhere is there a verse that specifically predicts anything about God becoming man, being called Jesus, dying for our sins on the cross, and rising again three days later. God's track record with prophecy is abysmal. If you're going to give him the same benefit of doubt as Madame Cricket and her 800 number, does that mean Madame Cricket is a god too?

Answered prayer

Theists claim that prayer works but it doesn't. Prayer has some physical and emotional benefits; it's like meditation—comforting, calming. That's a good thing but it isn't evidence that what you are praying to exists. Prayer can help sick people because it makes them feel better, that's all. It has nothing to do with the validity of their beliefs.

It says very clearly and plainly in the Bible that whatever you ask for in Jesus' name, you'll get. But it doesn't work so what happens? Apologists make excuses for why prayer doesn't work. It doesn't work because God is running the show not us. Sometimes the answer is no. But that's not what it says in the Bible. It says nothing about getting whatever you pray for unless God says no, or unless it's not the will of God. It says, "And whatever you ask in my name, I will do, so that the Father may be glorified in the Son. If you ask anything of me in my name, I will do it." (John 14: 13-14) Plain as day! But it's a lie, isn't it?

What about praying for a sick person to be healed? Theists do that all the time. It says in the Bible that if you pray over a sick person, God will heal him! No maybes, no "only if the answer is yes." It says, "Is anyone among you sick? He should summon the presbyters of the church, and they should pray over him and anoint him with oil in the name of the Lord, and the prayer of faith will save the sick person, and the Lord will raise him up." (James 5: 14-15) But it's a lie! Believers pray over sick people all the time and they die; so what do we get? We get apologists again saying the will of God takes precedent regardless of what it says in his book. God's will means sometimes the answer is no. In other words, prayer has no effect. If God wills you to be healed, you'll get better, if he doesn't, it was your time to go. If it's up to God to begin with, why did James tell people to pray? Why bother with the praying at all?

You can see why a rationalist won't accept that because someone prayed for something and got it a few times he has evidence for the existence of the god to whom he prayed.

Subjective experience

Humans are very strange; it's no wonder the practice of psychology exists. Figuring out the human psyche must be a daunting task indeed. Take the human penchant for thinking that everyone else thinks just like we do. People tend to believe that everyone has the same feelings, beliefs, and experiences as they themselves and yes, in a way, it's true; we are all human. We all do weird things and we share much in common as a species. Of course we do, but that doesn't mean that your subjective experience must be interpreted by everyone else the same way you interpret it.

Humans, it seems, live in their own worlds; they are self-centered creatures, tending to assume that other people would believe what they do, if they only had the same subjective experiences. What is difficult for the believer to accept is that atheists do have the same experiences; they just interpret their origin and meaning differently. Being self-centered also means thinking that what you believe to be true *is* necessarily true and if others don't accept it as true it is their fault, somehow, or their denial of the truth.

The believer experiences feelings of a presence, a loving energy, and he interprets them as emanating from whichever god he happens to believe in by upbringing or culture. The atheist has these feelings and interprets them naturally, as expected results of the chemical reactions in the human brain, as feelings of immense joy or peace while meditating, perhaps, on some particular beauty or wonder.

I think that if one god did exist and wanted his presence known, a subjective experience of him would be exactly the same for each individual and there would be an objective reality on which to base that experience—no incorrect interpretation would be possible. Deity, if it wanted to be known, would have an objective, real presence in this world, not just inside our hearts, souls or minds.

Theists say that they just know that God is there; they experience him, feel his presence, commune with him. But a person's subjective experience isn't evidence of anything beyond what that person believes he is experiencing. I accept the individual's story is true for him, but it isn't evidence. I believe that he is experiencing what he says he is, but I don't accept his interpretation of that experience. If I must accept the Christian experience of God as proof of God, he must not only accept the Muslim experience of Allah as proof of Allah, and the pagan experience of Goddess as proof of Goddess, but also my experience of no god as proof of no god.

The effects of belief

Christians tell me that when you become a Christian, your life is changed. People have won battles against drugs, crime and, of course, sexual perversity after turning their lives over to Christ. That's evidence, they say, that God is real. Well, not really. It's evidence that these people found something to believe in that gave them courage and hope and support. That's the power of belief...and the power of a supportive community. It isn't evidence of the validity of the belief itself. What about people who turn to paganism and Wicca and their lives are better for it? You can't claim evidence for your god and deny the same evidence for others. What about those of us who turned our lives around without the help of any supernatural beliefs or spiritualism? Is that proof that there are no gods?

The numbers game

The believer generally assumes that because the vast majority of humanity believes in some kind of god, there must be some kind of god. They claim that humans are conscious of God because God exists or that if no god existed, humans would not have an awareness (subjective experience) of or consciousness of God. Believers haven't shown that belief in God is inborn—that it isn't a learned behavior.

Majority god-belief is not evidence. The fact that most people believe in a god only means that most humans believe in a god. It has nothing to do with whether or not there is a real entity toward which that the belief points.

The spread of Christianity

Finally, Christians tell me that the massive and quick spread of Christianity is evidence that it is the true religion; but that's only evidence that people adopted Christianity, not that Christianity is more valid than any other religion. If it were, the fact that Christianity isn't the only religion in the world, or that most people are not Christians, should then be evidence that it isn't true.

❧❧❧❧

The above evidence for God is not relevant to the rationalist. We have different standards for evidence. I have been told that I can't see or experience the evidence in a manner that will allow me to accept it until I am filled with a holy spirit. That means that I can't believe it until I believe it and that you accept the evidence only because you believe it, while I can't accept it because I don't. That seems a bit silly to me.

I try to imagine what life would be like if a god did exist. If the god of the Bible existed, I imagine life would be just like it was in those stories. God would be evident, everywhere, every day interacting with his creation in a real and objective way. But, God has disappeared; he is hidden. He exists now only in the subjective experience of those who believe in him. No one has any real evidence for God. People who believe he exists are stuck with exactly that: belief. You have to just believe it, because you can never know for certain. That's just not good enough for me.

Chapter Seven

The Making of a Christian

I don't have a problem with the idea of some unknown cause bringing about the universe. The deists are fine by me. I don't believe it; it doesn't seem plausible; but I suppose it's possible. I often wondered, however, how a person gets from "I don't know how it all began" to Christianity. Granted, many, if not most, Christians were indoctrinated with the belief from a very early age. Reasoning their way to Christianity was unnecessary and only the opportunity to take a rational look at their beliefs would cause them to apply it. Once applied, however, what line of reasoning leads a person to Jesus? I can't pretend to know the path that all Christians took to arrive at their beliefs but I was honored to have one Christian of my acquaintance share his reasoning with me and I would like to outline it here. It begins with the question of the origin of the universe and ends with Jesus rising from the dead.

First Cause deism

The First Cause argument states simply that the universe is not infinite, it had a beginning therefore it had a cause. That cause is God. The problem with this argument is immediately evident: if the universe had a cause, we don't know what that cause was—no one knows. When you call it God, you assume quite a bit and you assume it without any evidence. It is a mere assertion.

Theists look around the world and say, "I just can't believe all this came about by mere chance so there must be a guiding hand; there must be a god." But, this world operates on basic natural laws about which we are learning all the time. It wasn't mere chance. Most importantly, just because you can't imagine that the world came about naturally doesn't mean it didn't.

Some scientists theorize that time and space had no beginning, that the universe is cyclic, eternally expanding and retracting. The universe is, then, eternal. Theists say that is impossible, because an infinite amount of time could never be traversed to arrive at the present. In other words, if the universe has an infinite past, you'd never get to now. At first glance that argument made a little bit of sense, but something nagged at me every time I heard it. When you talk about traversing a certain amount of time, aren't you presupposing a temporal starting point at which to begin traversing? If the universe is eternal, I don't think we can talk about traversing time. I don't think time would work in quite the way we humans consider it. The same argument, it seems to me, works against God. If God has an infinite past, how could he have gotten to the point at which he created the universe? But, for some reason, arguments used against nonbelief are never considered valid by theists when they are used against God.

Many scientists theorize that there was a moment before which time did not exist and after this singularity, time began and the universe existed. This does not answer the question of what may have existed, if anything, prior to that singularity. Theists want to say God, but that is just a guess.

Let's agree for the sake of argument that the universe had a beginning. Christians tell me that everything has a cause. If you regress through the causes of everything you eventually come to the First Cause which, strangely enough, need not have a cause. Why can this First Cause be uncaused? The answer is obvious: evasion. The problem Christians have been plagued with is this question: If everything has a cause, what caused God? This will not do. So, they claim that the First Cause had no cause—an assertion with no reasoning behind it. If gods can be uncaused, why can't the universe?

A clever ruse to get around the problem is to claim that everything that *begins to exist* has a cause. God did not begin to exist therefore, God needn't have a cause. This is nonsense. If you put everything that begins to exist in one basket and everything that is eternal in another, what have you got in that eternal basket? Only God. All the theist has done with this argument is create a special case for his god and then act as if it proves something.

Some Christians claim that only a created universe makes sense. They say that man has questions such as, "How did humans get here? Why am I here? What is my purpose?" Only if there is a god, they say, do those questions have answers. I don't agree. If there is no god, here are the answers: We evolved; probably no reason in particular; and, you probably don't have one. What the Christian is looking for is not an answer, but an answer that he likes. The Christian who uses this argument is really just saying that he likes the thought of the universe being created because it answers certain questions in the manner he prefers. That's fine, really but, it doesn't mean that there is a creator. Claiming that the universe is created simply because man has questions is putting man at the center of it and saying that supporting mankind is the purpose of the universe. Pretty egotistical, don't you think?

The Christian asserts that the universe had a cause and, we call that cause God. So far, he's a deist and he has made a leap of faith to get there; he has no evidence that there was a First Cause and no evidence that it was a god. He merely asserts these things and believes them to be true.

God's plan

The next step is the assumption that God had a plan. If there is a god and he created the universe, he must have had a reason. Again, this is just an assertion, just an idea that people have. People don't do things without reason, they say, so why would God? Except, of course, that people do things all the time without thinking and without real cause; and why should a god be anything like a person anyway? We've taken another leap of faith in assuming that our god had a reason for creating the universe and a plan for mankind.

God's revelation

Now we assume that if God had a plan and a reason for creating humans, he would want to let us know what that plan is. Not only is this another mere assertion without any evidence to back it up, but the Christian assumes that the Bible is that revelation. All other holy books and revelations of gods past and present are false, only their book and their god is the real one.

The only reason I have been given for preference of the Bible over the revelations of other gods is that the Bible and Christianity are the best explanation of the world and human nature. That isn't true, of course, except in the mind of the person who prefers the Bible and it's highly unlikely that Christians have studied all of the ancient pagan religions as well as Judaism, Islam, Hinduism, Shinto, and Buddhism. It is more likely that most Christians believe the Bible is the only word of the only god because they've been taught that and live in a society that supports it. These are not good reasons for accepting it as true.

The son of God

Then of course we arrive at Christianity after our long line of assertions. If the universe had a beginning, if there is a god, if he had a plan, if he revealed that plan, if that plan is the Bible, then Jesus is the son of God and rose from the dead.

⚬⚬⚬

That's it. That's what makes a Christian a Christian as far as I have learned; but it's all quicksand. It's based on nothing but assertion after assertion. Is there any evidence for any of it? No. I have heard Christians make lots of claims for the validity of their religion. There are two reasons for this. For most, they have not investigated the claims for themselves. That is the reason why the vast majority of believers accept the Bible as the word of God and the historicity of Jesus. They've been taught that it is true and have no reason to question it. For those who have investigated and still believe, it is because their standard of evidence is different from the skeptics'. They accept the supernatural world view, subjective experience, feelings, other people's testimony and errant views of history as evidence for what they believe.

What makes an atheist? At what point do atheists and believers part ways? At the very first assertion the rationalist balks. We don't know how the universe and our existence came to be. No one knows. Rationalists are not willing to accept an assertion—that there must be a creator—without adequate evidence. Theists and non-theists part ways as soon as theists start creating the world view that suits them.

Evidence for Jesus

Most Christians, and even many non-Christians, believe that Jesus was a historical figure. I accepted it too, for much of my life, until I began investigating the facts for myself. I am no longer convinced that such a person ever existed. I imagine most Christians believe that Jesus really existed because it says so in the Bible, and they have been taught to value the Bible as truth. And they've been told he existed by their families, churches and culture. There is no reason for them to doubt it. Even those Christians who accept that much of the Bible is allegory and symbolism, utilizes literary device and is error-prone because it was penned by men, still believe that the stories of Jesus are generally true.

I find it amusing that Paul stated explicitly that "every human being is a liar," (Romans 3:4) and then went on to teach us about Jesus. The entire Bible was put to paper by men. If all men are liars, how can you believe any of it? For people who are more skeptical of the Bible, its benefit as evidence for anything is doubtful. While the New Testament stories can be considered sources of information regarding the existence of Jesus, we must determine how valid they are as evidence. And, we must look outside the Bible for unbiased corroboration.

Contemporary extra-Biblical evidence for Jesus is nonexistent. The way I see it is this: here is the son of the one and only god come to Earth to tell us the good news, that if we only believe in him, we are forgiven of our sin and can go to Heaven after we die. Surely this is a most wondrous event, the most miraculous, fabulous, awe-inspiring, loving event in our world's history! So, why are there no mentions of it in any historical writings of the period? Why didn't anyone notice until a few years later when the writings of Paul circulated and a few years after that when the gospels were written? God became man and died for our salvation and nobody noticed. The reason is clear: incarnating, resurrecting, miracle-performing gods, saviors, Christs and Messiahs ran rampant at the time. Nobody noticed because the story wasn't special.

Christians will attempt to prove it happened by pointing to several historians of the time for verification, but they all fall short. The most often cited is Josephus, a Jewish historian who was born in 37 CE and died about 100 CE. Immediately Josephus can be discounted as a contemporary of Jesus as he was born after Jesus was supposedly killed. Anything he wrote would be nothing more than hearsay from followers of the Christian religion.

Josephus is cited in two places in *The Jewish Antiquities*. The first is the Testimony of Flavius, most often cited and most obviously fraudulent. The second is a reference to James as the brother of Jesus which is generally considered legitimate. I challenge everyone to read the Testimony of Flavius—not just the paragraph in question, but the entire sections before and after it. The paragraph about Jesus abruptly interrupts the discourse. It is so obviously a later insertion that has nothing to do with the original text that one might fail to understand the passion with which Christians claim it as proof. But the manner in which misinformation, misquotes and outright lies are spread through the Christian community and are repeated again and again tells us why: it works. People prefer to simply believe what they're told rather than research and study for themselves.

I understand that Christians would appreciate confirmation of their beliefs, but it's just not there. No scholar worth his merit would claim the passage in Josephus is anything beyond forgery. The only difference is that some believe the entire paragraph to be interpolation while others claim that only the words about Jesus as Christ, miracle worker and resurrected were. The fact that Eusebius (about 260-before 341 CE), an early apologist, didn't mention the passage in Josephus at all is further evidence of its lack of authenticity. Regardless, both passages cited in Josephus as evidence were written too late to be anything beyond hearsay.

All other writings offered as evidence for the historicity of Jesus are too vague to be considered evidence and are written too late to be considered confirmation of anything beyond people's belief in his existence.

Tacitus (55-120 CE) wrote a passage in his *Annals* some eighty years after the supposed death of Jesus. In it, he explained that the belief that Christians were responsible for the great fire at Rome in 64 CE could not be dispelled. He called the founder of the religion Christus and claimed he was put to death by Pontius Pilate. This proves nothing beyond the fact that Christianity existed and its founder was believed to have been a historical person.

A snippet written by Suetonius (75-150 CE), in *The Deified Claudius*, written too late to be evidence, merely mentions a Chrestus expelled, with his followers, by Rome. There is no confirmation that this Chrestus is Jesus. If Chrestus does mean Christus, it would still only mean one of the many Messiahs running around Rome at the time was expelled. Christus, in Latin, simply means Messiah and there were plenty of them handy in those days.

Pliny the Younger (62-113 CE) wrote a letter to the Emperor Trajan in Rome in 113 CE in which he discusses Christians, and Emperor Hadrian (117-138 CE) wrote a letter to the Asian proconsul about Christians—both too late to mean anything except that Christians existed at that time.

Thallus is often claimed to have been a witness to the "darkness" that occurred when Jesus was killed. Solar eclipses were a common claim at the deaths of kings or other historic events in the Mediterranean. The only citations of darkness at the time of Jesus' death in the New Testament can be found in Mark 15:33, Luke 23:44 and Matthew 27:45. No other New Testament authors, including Paul, make the claim. According to the Gospels, the darkness occurred during a full moon (impossible for a solar eclipse) and lasted three hours, covering the whole Earth. It is very telling that the only witness outside Biblical testimony to mention this incredible event is a pagan historian for whom the only information we have comes exclusively from early Christian apologists. His name and what he wrote come from the apologists beginning in the second century. We can't be sure when Thallus wrote. Thallus was first mentioned by Theophilus in about 180 CE. It is most likely that Thallus wrote sometime in the second century and was not a witness to the crucifixion.

In the year 221 CE the Christian apologist Julius Africanus claimed that Thallus explained the darkness at the time of Jesus' death as an eclipse, an opinion with which Africanus disagreed. That is all we know! To what eclipse did Thallus refer? Did he, himself, ascribe it to Jesus' death or was that assumption made by Africanus? We don't know because none of Thallus' writings exist!

What about Phlegon, the Greek freedman of the emperor Hadrian? A few modern apologists still trot him out as evidence of the darkness at Jesus' death. But just as with Thallus, the writings cited by apologists no longer exist; they are merely quoted by early Christians Julius Africanus and Origen. Phlegon was born too late, no surprise there, in about 80 CE and he wrote in the second century. He could not have been a witness even had we his own words to make the claim.

More interesting are the fragments of Phlegon's writings that were preserved. Phlegon, it seems, loved tales of the fantastic. From his *Olympiads*, a sixteen volume work, one chapter that survives is called

On Marvels. It's all about ghosts, prophecies and monstrous births, an accounting of ancient superstitions. His credulous claims include a dismembered head that tells the future, a man who changes to a woman and back, and men giving birth. This is the historian apologists turn to for verification of the existence of Jesus?

The thing about Thallus and Phlegon and the darkness is that both of them are quoted as calling the darkness an eclipse—a three-hour long eclipse. This eclipse happened during the lifetimes of Seneca and the elder Pliny. Seneca was a philosopher and writer who lived from 4 BCE until 65 CE, the perfect time frame in which to remark about a historical Jesus and a three-hour eclipse. Pliny the Elder (23-79 CE) wrote, among other things, a 37-book compilation called *The Natural History* which he completed in 77 CE. His *Natural History* covered a great number of subjects, including astronomy. Neither of these Roman intellectuals mentions Jesus, Christianity or a three-hour eclipse.

Another source offered by Christians for the historicity of Jesus is the *Talmud*, compiled between 70 and 200 CE. But this mention only says a Yeshua was hanged on the eve of Passover. The reference is too vague and too late to mean anything.

Mara Bar-Serapion is sometimes referred to as evidence for Jesus, but as usual, he wrote too late (between 70 and 200 CE) to mean anything beyond the existence of the cult. Bar-Serapion wrote from prison to his son persuading him to emulate great teachers of the past, of whom Jesus was one.

And finally, Lucian, a second-century Greek satirist poked some fun at Christianity, stating that the Christian law-giver was crucified. Lucian was born about 120 CE and enjoyed ratting out the numerous pagan sects for their gullibility. Therefore, say Christians, the fact that Lucian said, even in satire, that Jesus was crucified must mean he really was. If Lucian knew Jesus was not a historical figure killed under Pilate, he'd have said so. Possibly, but, there was no way for Lucian to have known such a thing as he was born in the second century and his knowledge of Christianity would come primarily from its sects. It's also possible that Lucian didn't doubt Jesus as historical because he wouldn't have been the only real man going about the countryside supposedly casting out demons, healing people, and claiming a connection with the spiritual world.

There are more serious problems with these supposed references to Jesus besides having been written too late to confirm his existence but, because they are so easily made unacceptable as evidence for the historicity of Jesus, I needn't elaborate on their other issues.

There is no outside corroborating evidence for the existence of Jesus. Even the stories told of him in the Bible and the Gnostic gospels found at Nag Hammadi were written years after Jesus' supposed death. Christians say that there is little evidence that people questioned the historicity of Jesus or what the New Testament writers claimed of him. There is some, but I agree there is little evidence of detractors at the time just as there is little evidence of historicity. But one thing we know about the history of Christianity is that once it gained power, its leaders began a systematic cleansing of all opposition, including the various sects of its own religion that didn't agree with the orthodoxy. It is not a mystery to me that little anti-Christian documentation exists today.

If we take all we have regarding Jesus, we might assume he did exist, but was just another charlatan or a misunderstood philosopher. I believed for a long time that Jesus was a wise man, a great teacher. After reading the Bible I thought differently. Some study of history helped me to understand that Jesus was not the only god incarnate worshiped at the time, nor, if he existed, the only person making the Messianic claims he supposedly did. After I read about the correlations between the pagan mystery religions and the Gnostics, suddenly Christianity made sense to me. When taken literally it is a confusing mesh of contradiction and absurdity; when looked at through paganism, it has meaning. If Jesus existed as a man, the religion built around him was absorbed from the various pagan myths abundant in his lifetime.

❈❈❈❈

It is not a foregone conclusion that there is a god, that he had a plan, that he revealed that plan, that the Christian Bible is that plan nor that Jesus actually existed and was the son of God. In fact, the evidence is nonexistent for all of those claims. They are all suspect, doubtful, mere assertions. The nonbeliever's position is not without merit.

When Christians accept the assumptions necessary to reach their conclusion they do so by faith. I am willing to accept that as their reason for believing. In my opinion, they should admit that they believe by faith alone and leave the attempts at reasonable justification aside. In order to claim that belief in Christianity is reasonable and based on evidence, it is necessary for the Christian to defend the indefensible and to, as a result, make derogatory claims regarding the opposing side—atheists. In order to continue to assert they have objective evidence to support their belief (which if true would render belief unnecessary) they must try to put atheists into the position of denial of their supposedly obvious truth. If they had evidence to support their beliefs, the debate would be over; but because they have none, they eventually turn to demonizing the enemy. As soon as the disparaging claims are made—atheists are willful, blind, and immoral—it is apparent that Christianity has no solid base on which to stand.

So, why don't Christians admit theirs is a faith that can't be defended? Because when they do that, they will have to concede that nonbelief is reasonable and acceptable. They will be forced to tolerate it, to admit they could be wrong, and to allow that atheists are just as moral and decent as they are. They will have no excuse not to separate religion and government completely, to cease the posting of religious symbols and phrases on government property, to stop trying to get everyone else's children to pray to their god in public schools, and to stop trying to have their creation myth taught as if it were factual.

Christians can not do those things, at least not yet. Too many of them are grounded in self-righteous bigotry and the rest are simply going along for the ride, secure in the belief that they are right and there is nothing wrong with forcing their religion on others. I hear there are more tolerant Christians out there who do acknowledge the rights of nonbelievers. If that's true, perhaps a more liberal Christianity will one day grow out of the ashes of fundamentalism. We can only hope.

Chapter Eight

The Making of a Religion

Once I realized I was atheist, I looked at the Christian theology with a skeptical eye and wondered why anyone would believe it. To be honest, at first I thought people must be either ignorant, or they didn't really believe it at all. I thought, come on, they really know deep down that there isn't a god. Funny, they thought the same thing about me, that deep down, I must really believe there is a god. Instead of butting heads over the idea, I figured that Christians who professed to really believe in God must really believe. And as you would expect, when I began to correspond with Christians, I found that most were not ignorant at all. Many very intelligent people believe in God and believe that Jesus rose from the dead.

The next logical question was, why? Why would anyone believe that a god exists who created humanity especially for the purpose of worshiping and adoring him? Who would believe that this great, superior, supreme, being would torture parts of his creation for not believing in him? What sort of creature would do something like that? To me, of course, only an egotistical monster would. To the fundamentalist Christian, God loves us! He loves me but he's going to send me to Hell.

Granted, not all Christians believe Hell is a place of torment and not all even believe that Hell exists. Most of the Christians I interact with, however, do believe in Hell as a punishment for all manner of sins, not the least of which is nonbelief. They are quick to defend their all-loving

god, however, when I protest such behavior on his part. "God isn't
sending you to Hell, you're sending yourself there," I am told.

But God created Hell. Didn't God set up the garden, the temptation
of the tree? Didn't he let the serpent have a go at those newly created
innocents Adam and Eve? Didn't God set up the whole scheme, the
whole plan? Knowing full well what would happen? He's terribly irre-
sponsible, incredibly stupid, or just plain mean.

Why do people believe that the stories in the Bible are at all factual? The most recent research exposes the Old Testament stories of the
Hebrews as untrue. Archaeological evidence since the Seventies does
not confirm the Bible in history, but shows instead that it is not reliable
history at all. The Old Testament is nothing more than the exaggerated
stories of a nomadic people in need of a great heritage. They simply
created one.

You can find, with a study of the *Gilgamesh* epic and the *Egyptian
Book of the Dead*, that the story of Genesis is borrowed heavily from
Egyptian and Babylonian myth. The New Testament stories of Jesus
are also born out of earlier and current mythical ideas. Jesus most likely
was, as the evidence suggests, a Jewish version of the prevailing pagan
gods. You can read the evidence of the similarities between the myths
of Osiris-Dionysus, Bacchus, Adonis and Jesus in many available
books.

The well-read Biblical Christian will tell you, most likely, one of
two things regarding the fact that earlier myths resemble theirs. Either
the earlier myths arose out of man's yearning for God, a precursor of
the True Word of God, or Satan planted all those earlier similar myths
to confuse us. Of course, there are Christians who will simply deny any
correlation between other myths and Christianity. This is a difficult position to hold in light of the early Church fathers' defense against their
critics who pointed out the similarities.

Joseph Wheless, in *Forgery in Christianity* (Kessinger), quotes
Justin Martyr in his *Dialogue with Trypho* as saying:

> For when they tell that Bacchus, son of Jupiter, was begot-
> ten by [Jupiter's] intercourse with Semele, and that he was the
> discoverer of the vine; and when they relate, that being torn in
> pieces, and having died, he rose again, and ascended to Heaven;
> and when they introduce wine into his mysteries, do I not per-
> ceive that [the devil] has imitated the prophecy announced by

the patriarch Jacob, and recorded by Moses?...And when he [the devil] brings forward Aesculapius as the raiser of the dead and healer of all diseases, may I not say in this matter likewise he has imitated the prophecies about Christ?...And when I hear that Perseus was begotten of a virgin, I understand that the deceiving serpent counterfeited this also.

Wheless also quotes Tertullian, Bishop of Carthage (c.160-220 CE) who claimed: "You [Pagans] say we worship the sun; so do you." You can find translations of the early Christian writers, including Justin Martyr and Tertullian, online at www.earlychristianwritings.com.

I don't accept the explanations that similarities between Christianity and paganism are due to Satan's handiwork or human yearning for God. Those sound very much like poor excuses made by people who simply choose to believe their own myths are true while others are false.

The Christian defense that there are no real similarities between their theology and pagan myths is based on the supposition that Christianity is unique. Yes, they say, you might find some vague similarities, but no other religions are exactly like Christianity. No other gods came to Earth and died exactly in the way Jesus did or for the same reasons. This defense belies an ignorance of human cultural practices.

No one claims that Christianity was taken wholesale from another religious belief. No one claims that someone else's theology was adopted and simply renamed. That's not how cultural borrowing works. Humans adopt bits and pieces of other cultures, taking what they like and leaving what they don't. Then they add to it to make it uniquely theirs. All religions are unique.

The skeptic claim is that pagan gods incarnated, died and were resurrected. The ideas were current, floating around, ready to be adopted and made into new religions. The gods most often cited as similar to Jesus are Osiris and Dionysus of Egypt and Greek theology. But some other gods incarnate worshiped at the time were Inanna, Tammuz, Zalmoxis and Mithras. The following is a brief look at these pagan gods and their similarities to Jesus.

Osiris

The cult of Osiris was in existence from 3000 BCE. His annual passion play, commemorating the events of his life, death and resurrection, was celebrated until 400 CE. Osiris was an Egyptian god. When he was born to Rhea a voice was heard to proclaim that the lord of creation was born. Osiris established laws for Egypt then set out to civilize other lands. In his absence, Isis, his wife and sister, ruled Egypt. When Osiris returned to Egypt, the evil Set (or Typhon) tricked him into getting into a coffin. Set locked him in and tossed the coffin into the Nile.

Isis cut a lock of hair in grief over her husband's death and sought out his body. Once she found it, she sought out her son Horus. But Set found the coffin while Isis was away and cut Osiris' body into fourteen pieces, hiding them throughout the land. Isis found all the body parts, pieced them together and Osiris was resurrected and rose to reign eternally in Heaven.

So, Osiris was a god who at one time possessed human form to rule the Earth. He was killed, resurrected and is now ruler of the dead in Heaven.

Dionysus

Dionysus was a Greek god born of a human mother. His Roman counterpart, Bacchus, was spoken of by Justin Martyr as quoted earlier. He actually had two lives, one divine and the other mortal; he was resurrected twice. First, Zeus (Jupiter in the Roman pantheon) came to Persephone, a goddess, disguised as a serpent and she bore Dionysus as Zagreus. Jealous Hera, Zeus' wife, provoked the Titans into killing Dionysus. They tore him into seven pieces, boiled and ate him. But his heart was rescued. Zeus used a potion made from Dionysus' heart to impregnate Semele, princess of Thebes. Hera, jealous again, tricked Semele into asking Zeus to reveal himself as a god, at which moment his divine fire incinerated Semele and she was cast to the underworld. Her fetus (Dionysus), who was said to have danced in his mother's womb, was taken out of her ashes by Zeus and sewn into his thigh until he could be born. So it was said he was twice born or born again.

The cult of Dionysus had spread to Italy by the third century BCE. It reached Rome in 496 BCE and became very popular there by the second century BCE. In the earliest festivals celebrating the life of Dionysus, believers tore apart a live animal and drank its blood, believing they were partaking of the god's body and blood, sharing in the essence of the god. By the mid third century his followers called him the Redeemer; he was the god of wine. He was said to have risen from the dead each year to rule the winter months and was celebrated as rising in March and dying in December.

So, Dionysus was a god popular in Rome, born of a goddess, killed and resurrected via birth of a mortal mother, born twice, the Redeemer, celebrated in the eating of his body and drinking of his blood, and in his death in December and his rebirth or resurrection in March.

Inanna

Inanna was a Babylonian goddess worshiped long before Ishtar (Babylonian), Tammuz (son lover of Ishtar) or Dionysus. Inanna was the Queen of Heaven and Earth who entered the underworld upon hearing the cries of her sister Ereshkigal. Before entering the first gate, she told her servant Ninshubur to wait three days and three nights for her; if Inanna failed to return, Ninshubur was to seek help. At each of the seven gates to the underworld, Inanna was forced to part with one of her signs of dominion and power until she was naked before her sister. The judges of the underworld ruled against her for trying to assume power in the underworld and she was killed by being hung from a hook on the wall.

Meanwhile, Ninshubur contacted the God of Wisdom, who created two beings from the dirt under his fingernails; the beings descended into the underworld, healed Ereshkigal of her pain (some sources say due to childbirth), and as a prize, asked for the body of Inanna. Inanna was resurrected and returned to Heaven.

The Semitic goddess, Ishtar, replaced Inanna during the decline of the Sumerian kingdom. Ishtar is considered to be an incarnation of Inanna.

So, Inanna was a god who descended twice, first from Heaven to Earth, then to the underworld; she was judged, crucified, and resurrected.

Tammuz

Tammuz was worshiped by the Phoenicians, Hebrews, Canaanites, Babylonians and Assyrians by his title, Adonai, meaning Lord. Sumerians worshiped him as Dumuzi, the vegetation god and husband of Inanna, who showed the people how to approach the gods.

Tammuz died young in the winter and descended into Hell or the underworld. Through his death and rebirth, the fields and flocks were recovered. Women were required to weep and mourn for his return to ensure the rebirth of the Earth. The prophet Ezekial, chapter eight verse fourteen, expresses his frustration with the continued practice in the Old Testament. The cult of Tammuz spread to Phrygia and Greece where he was worshiped as Attis and Adonis.

So, Tammuz was Lord, died young in winter, was mourned by women, descended to hell and was resurrected in spring.

Zalmoxis

We have very little information on the worship of Zalmoxis. Herodotus wrote of him in his *Histories* of 440 BCE. He said that the Thracians worshiped Zalmoxis and believed that when they died, they went to live eternally with him. The Greeks claimed, according to Herodotus, that Zalmoxis was a man, a former slave of Pythagoras who was freed and after amassing wealth returned to his own country to school his people in the arts of civilization. Zalmoxis, they said, built a huge hall in which he feasted with the elite of his countrymen all the while building an underground chamber. He taught his doctrine of eternal life and then disappeared, descending into his chamber. For three years his people mourned him as dead. In the fourth year, he rose out of his chamber and the people then believed his doctrine.

So, in Zalmoxis we have a story of a god/man who descended into a tomb of sorts and then arose out of it, and preached a doctrine of eternal life.

Mithras

The Roman cult of Mithras was very secret. What we know about it today comes from outsiders such as early Church Fathers writing about it in order to attack it, philosophers appealing to its doctrines, and artifacts from the thousands of underground temples dedicated to the god.

Roman Mithraism arose at about the same time Christianity did causing Christians to claim that we can't be sure whether Christianity is copied from Mithraism or vice versa. But the earliest record we have of the pagan cult is 67 BCE when Plutarch wrote about a band of pirates in Cilica practicing the secret rites of Mithras. Thus, Mithraism in Rome predates Christianity, unless the Christians would like to change their time line. The earliest physical evidence dates to the first century

CE and Mithraism was at its height in popularity in the third century. It was eventually eclipsed by Christianity and exterminated in the purge of all religious practices deemed heretical.

Roman Mithraism, however, is related to, and has its roots in, the Persian god Mithra, at first a minor deity, but later a full-fledged god worshiped very much like Jesus. The similarities between Mithra and Jesus are numerous and amazing. Both were born of a virgin mother on December 25, performed miracles, and were known as the "light of the world." They were both considered saviors of mankind, were both killed and resurrected. Mithraism and Christianity are both based on the dual nature of good and evil, and incorporate baptism, a sacred banquet, and resurrection.

⁕⁕⁕⁕

These aren't the only gods similar to Jesus, but the point isn't to try to figure out which gave rise to the Christian god. They all lent ideas to the surrounding cultures. The point, which is so obvious and yet so quickly dismissed by Christians, is that at the time Christianity had its beginnings, people readily accepted gods incarnating as human men, suffering, dying for our salvation, and resurrecting. None were exactly like Jesus—all of them were unique. But Jesus was nothing new; the ideas surrounding him were not original.

People at the time were very superstitious. They believed that men could be gods. Even the Bible shows us, in Acts, chapter fourteen, that the people of Lystra believed Paul and Barnabas to be Zeus and Hermes incarnated. Gods becoming men was not an original idea. People also prayed to statues, believing they would be healed by them; miracle workers abounded; they followed every new Messiah, sometimes to their deaths. To characterize the people of that time as rational, sensible people who were convinced despite themselves of the (capital T) Truth by the miraculous life, death and resurrection of Jesus is simply inappropriate, if not disingenuous.

To claim that Christianity is unique is not saying much. There were other gods before Jesus who did miraculous things. Why should we believe the stories of the others were false and Christianity's is true? Because it is the only story that is still believed by large numbers of people today? The number of people who believe something or how long the idea survives has no bearing on its validity. The fact that the main ideas of Christianity were accepted by pagans in various forms before the story of Jesus erupted is proof that Christianity is not special and evidence that it is not any more valid than its older, pagan versions.

⋇⟡⋇

Ancient people all over the world worshiped the Sun. They watched its rising and setting location travel from north to south throughout the year and experienced the changes its path produced on Earth. The winter solstice is that time when, because of the tilt of the Earth, your hemisphere is leaning farthest from the Sun so that daylight time is very short and the Sun's path is at the lowest arc of its travels. Solstice means "Sun-standing-still." The Earth seems on the brink of death; the Sun seems to be slowly disappearing. The warming, life-giving light may die out altogether. Without the intervention of Man, his supplications and ceremonial offerings, the Sun may not turn again, retrace its path, and renew the Earth. The winter solstice has been celebrated as the annual birth of various Sun gods for thousands of years.

The Sun begins its northward path again at the solstice in late December (winter solstice in the Northern Hemisphere; summer solstice in the Southern) and finally, the daylight and nighttime hours become equal. The Sun is midway through its path to the north, at the spring or vernal equinox, when Earth is thrust into rebirth. It rises again from the dearth of winter.

This is the origin of Christianity—of all religion. Christians aren't worshiping the son of God; they are worshiping the Sun god who is born in December and resurrects the Earth in spring. Jesus isn't coming back some time in the future; he returns every year. It was only the determination of a small sect of early followers of the Christ cult to claim their Sun god was actually the promised Messiah that confused the issue and led to the belief that Jesus was a historical figure. And because he failed to do what the Messiah was supposed to do, his death and resurrection were reinterpreted to point to a future, physical return. Because of that, Christians no longer worship Jesus as the original pagan, Jewish, Sun god; they now worship a supposedly real man/god who will return, not at each winter solstice, but in the future. They worship a vengeful god created by an oppressed Jewish population. They have, in essence, destroyed the beauty of the religion.

Chapter Nine

Morality

If the Bible and my brain are both the work of the same Infinite God, whose fault is it that the book and my brain do not agree?
—Robert G. Ingersoll

"Where do you get your morals?"

That's the question I get most often, as if morals are bought and sold at a shop somewhere and being an atheist is like being an anti-shopper so how can I have any morals? My answer to the question has never been accepted by any theist. It is this: same place you do. I get my morals from my family, community, society and culture. They are taught to me from birth. I learned some better and more quickly than others. I didn't learn some until later in life. Some of us never learn all of them. Some of us learn about morality but something is wrong with our wiring and we don't feel the guilt and shame or, more important, empathy necessary to keep us abiding by the moral laws of our society.

Theists are repelled at the thought that we get our morals from our culture. That would mean that morality is (gasp!) subjective and situational. They say "situational ethics" as if it's a disgusting concept and not what's been going on for millennia. And worse, they confuse situational and subjective ethics with individual ethics. They make statements like, if there is no absolute morality, we can all just do whatever we want. Christians who say things like that belie their ignorance of society and culture, not to mention ethics and morality.

People are inculcated with the morality of their culture and community. Yes, they make individual decisions; that's why people still steal and cheat. But the more unfavorably certain actions are looked upon by the greater society, the harder it is for a person to commit those acts. That's why you have fewer people murdering than you do lying. Committing acts deemed atrocious by society requires a lack of the fundamental emotions necessary to moral behavior, such as empathy and shame, often producing an extreme psychological rift between the individual and society; in other words, a psychosis.

Christians can rail against the morality of their society all they want but until they realize that the majority view is what creates the moral climate, they will only cause friction and discord. While morality is related to law, all the variations of personal moral values can't be legislated. Morality isn't something that can be forced on others; rather, we epitomize and exemplify our personal, familial, and community standard for others to judge. Discussion and persuasion, not attack and denigration, are the proper means to moral unity and understanding.

Christians try to force a morality onto society that doesn't fit because they claim we do not get our morals from our culture. So, I ask them, "Where do you get *your* morals?" They tell me we all get morals in two ways: God lays his moral law on our hearts and he outlined it in the Bible. I am also told God's moral law is absolute—unconditional and not limited by restrictions or exceptions. What are these absolute morals that God has outlined for humanity? There are none, if the truth be told. God's moral law is subjective and situational.

Is the moral law a separate and distinct set of laws, existing somewhere apart from God? Is it a set of laws that even God must obey? Is morality separate from God? If the moral law is separate from him, God is subject to it himself and must uphold it; but God fails to do so.

If murder is wrong, then he is guilty by his acts in the Old Testament. "I, on my part, am about to bring the flood waters on the earth, to destroy everywhere all creatures in which there is the breath of life; everything on earth shall perish." (Gen 6:17) "At midnight the Lord slew every first-born in the land of Egypt..." (Exod 12:29)

If lying is wrong, God is guilty of breaking the moral law. "So now, the Lord has put a lying spirit in the mouths of all these prophets of yours..." (1Kings 22:23) "And if the prophet be deceived and speak a word, I, the Lord, have deceived that prophet..." (Ezek 14:9)

Maybe that's what happened with Ezekiel and his false prophecy of Egypt? Or maybe the Bible is just stories that someone made up and God is not guilty of lying and murder at all. If so, how do you know what is true about God and what isn't? If these things are true of God, it means that he can break the moral law while holding us accountable to it; and we have no recourse in the matter. He's more powerful than we are and Might Makes Right.

However, I am told that God and moral law are one and the same; the moral code isn't above God because nothing is above God—he is supreme. God created the moral law or the law is part of his nature. That means that morality is subjective; it is subject to the will or nature of God.

If God says murder is good, murder is good because God is the author of morality. If God says infants being dashed to pieces (Isaiah 13:16) or bashing babies against rocks (Psalm 137:9) is good, then it is good because God says so. If God says that raping the virgins of your slaughtered enemy (Num 31:18) is good, then it is good. If God says that sending she-bears to maul young boys for teasing a bald priest (2Kings 2:24) is good, then it is good because God authored it. Whatever God calls good and moral, is, by definition, good and moral. What you or I may think of it is of no consequence. That's subjective morality. It emanates from the subjective mind of God.

I'm also told that God has written his law on my heart. God has instilled me with the knowledge of right and wrong; sort of like getting my morals as hand-me-downs instead of having to buy new. That is how I know that murder is wrong, even if God doesn't get the chance to tell me. That is why I am held responsible for my sin, even if I didn't know about it.

When I feel that slaughtering an entire enemy village—young boys, babies, the elderly, every living thing—except the virgin girls, is horrible, I think it's horrible because God has instilled me with a sense of right and wrong. Yet, what I find horrible is an act sanctioned, even commanded, by God in the Bible. Something God ordered, I find repugnant! How can this be?

Do you find any of the following morally wrong or bad in any way?
- ✓ a worldwide flood that kills babies, animals, everything (Gen 6, 7)
- ✓ human sacrifice (Lev 27: 28,29; Judges 11: 34, 39)
- ✓ a man offering his virgin daughters to a mob (Gen 19:8)

✓ the murder of the first born sons of an entire country (Exod 8)
✓ slavery (Exod 21: 2, 4-6, 20,21; Lev 25: 44-46)
✓ using women and casting them aside (Deut 21: 10-11, 13-14)
✓ taking captive virgins for your pleasure (Num 31)
✓ death penalty for idolatry and heresy (Exod 22:20)
✓ killing your family members for practicing another religion (Deut 13:6, 8-10)
✓ death penalty for menial labor on the Sabbath (Num 15: 32, 35-36)
✓ death penalty for all manner of silly things (OT laws)
✓ massacre of an entire people, capturing their virgins as booty, slaughter of helpless women and children (Num 31)
✓ massacring an entire people for something their ancestors did (1Sam 15:1-3,8)

All of these atrocities and more are sanctioned or commanded by the god of the Bible, the supposed author of my moral values. Here's the crux of the problem. By my moral standards, the Christian god is a mass murderer, a cruel tyrant, a torturer of frail and imperfect beings. Before I read the Bible, I had been told that God was love itself, that God loved me, that God so loved the world he gave his only son to die for my sins. But when I read the Bible, I didn't find that to be true. I found God to be disgusting.

If a person claims that any of those things I listed above are good for any reason whatsoever, they are immoral by the standards of Western society. I have heard people try to explain in what manner it was good for God to command those horrible deeds, good for all of us, good for God's people, even good for the victims. It's a disgusting display of the destructive power of belief.

I've been told that I do not, can not, have God's perspective but if I did, I would see that all God's actions are good and that once we are in God's presence we may be able to understand them. God had adequate reason to act the way he did and the outcome will be best for all. This sounds very much like the Ends Justify the Means, a concept I've heard degraded by Christians as immoral. I don't care what good may come of the murder of children, it is wrong under all circumstances. The ends can not justify the means, by my moral standard. I find it incredible that an omnipotent god could use no better means to reach his goal.

I've been told that my problem isn't with God; it's with Satan. Satan is causing me to misunderstand God, to see God's actions as evil. If I were a Christian and filled with the holy spirit, I'd see that God is good and all the bad things he did in the Old Testament were really good things.

I do not want to be filled with a spirit that would make me see horrible things as good. I don't think this holy spirit is a good spirit. How can it be right to see murdering young children (Num 31:17) as a good thing? I have to wonder who is really blind to the truth here.

I have been told that as the creator of humans, God has the right to do with us as he pleases, including ordering, committing, approving of, or not interfering with murder. This is blatant Might Makes Right thinking and I disagree. Humans are sentient beings. We reason, we feel joy and suffer pain. Once a deity creates sentient beings, his rights over them are severely limited.

How dare I judge God by my human morality? I dare because I do have moral standards and obviously mine are higher than the Bible god's. My standard of what is good and fair, loving and kind, forgiving and merciful is higher than that of the Christian god. If, as Christians claim, my morals came from God, something is amiss. If he gave me my moral standards, he is either above them and I am supposed to turn a blind eye to his violation of his own laws, or the god in the Bible isn't the god who created me and gave me my morals.

If God is indeed above the law, free to murder and torture humans, my moral standard tells me I must turn against him. Might does not make right. Murdering and torturing beings that are weaker than you are is not moral. I can not, will not, worship an immoral god.

Also, I must judge God. We all must judge God. According to Christian theology, God wants me to come to him of my own free will to worship, love and serve him. I can't choose God without first making a judgment about him. When Christians choose God and Jesus they make a judgment—they judge them worthy. I do not. Of course, I also don't believe that the god of the Bible exists, and it's a good thing he doesn't, the way I see it.

Morality and the Bible

[Slavery] was established by decree of Almighty God...it is sanctioned in the Bible, in both Testaments, from Genesis to Revelation...it has existed in all ages, has been found among the people of the highest civilization, and in nations of the highest proficiency in the arts.

—Jefferson Davis, President of the Confederate States of America

I've heard several Christians attempt to apologize for Jesus' lack of outrage against slavery by claiming that the institution didn't mean the same thing back then as it does today. By my moral standards, the indenture of one human being by another is bad; it is never good. Looking at the scriptures regarding slavery, detailing the punishments for beating or killing a slave or servant, it is apparent that slavery in ancient times was not much different than slavery throughout history. The attempts to tone it down, to make it seem that in Biblical times it was an honorable or caring situation is a blatant and immoral attempt to rationalize one's belief.

Others have told me that Jesus didn't speak out against slavery because the people of ancient times weren't capable of accepting such a dictum. That, to me, is ridiculous. Jesus told us to "be perfect, just as your Heavenly Father is perfect." (Matt 5:48) That is impossible to live by and yet, he told us to do it. Of course he would have told us to stop owning slaves if he thought we should.

Jesus was supposedly the son of God, the greatest prophet ever to walk the Earth and I am asked to believe he didn't bother to leave us with important rules. In actuality, he didn't need to. God left the explicit, exhausting rules for living in the Old Testament. Christians don't want to live by those laws so they imagine that Jesus somehow nullified them by "fulfilling the law." Yet, Jesus said he hadn't come to change the law one jot or tittle; "until Heaven and earth pass away, not the smallest letter or the smallest part of a letter will pass from the law." (Matt 5: 17-18)

Why don't Christians live by most of the Old Testament laws? I can think of three reasons: there is a passage somewhere in the Bible in which someone contradicts Jesus; the laws in the Old Testament are too tedious to follow; or, by today's standards many of those laws are immoral.

When I ask about the laws of God in the Bible, I'm generally offered the Ten Commandments but those traditional ten aren't the right ones. The traditional Ten Commandments are taken from Exodus, Chapter 20, though they aren't labeled as such in the text itself. The story goes like this: Moses led the people out of Egypt to Sinai and there went up the mountain to have a few words with Yahweh. Yahweh told Moses to remind the people how great a god he was, evidenced by his nastiness in dealing with the Egyptians, and to find out if they wanted to be his chosen people; the people agreed. Then Yahweh told

Moses to tell the people not to touch the mountain when he was on it (or they'd get stoned to death or shot with an arrow), not to sanctify themselves, and above all not to have intercourse with any women! After doing so, Moses went up the mountain again to get the commandments of God.

The traditional ten are laid out in Exodus Chapter 20, verses 2-17; but God didn't stop there. He continued in verses 22 through 25 and then Chapters 21, 22, and 23 with more laws—laws regarding slaves, personal injury, loans, social intercourse and religious practices. There aren't ten commandments; there are dozens.

The people down at the base of the mountain weren't behaving themselves and when Moses came down with his laws (for I suspect he wrote them himself and made the rule about not coming up the mountain while God was on it just to keep the riffraff from finding out the man behind the curtain was himself) he smashed them to the ground in anger. No matter, "The Lord said to Moses, 'Cut two stone tablets like the former that I may write on them the commandments which were on the former tablets that you broke.'" (Exodus 34: 1)

The problem is that the second set Yahweh gave Moses was not the same as the originals. God said: "But you, on your part, must keep the commandments I am giving you today." (Exodus 34: 11) And the real Ten Commandments are:

- ✓ Don't worship other gods or make covenants with people you defeat in war
- ✓ Don't make molten gods
- ✓ Keep the Feast of Unleavened Bread
- ✓ The first-born of your livestock and sons is to be given to God
- ✓ Work six days and rest on the seventh
- ✓ Keep the Feast of Weeks
- ✓ Don't sacrifice animals at the same time you sacrifice with leavened bread
- ✓ Don't keep the sacrifice of the Passover feast for the next day
- ✓ The first-fruits of the soil must be given to God
- ✓ Don't boil a kid in its mother's milk

I am at a loss as to why Christians don't claim these as the Ten Commandments. Either they don't actually read their Bible, or they just don't find these ten appealing. More importantly, if we follow any of the commandments issued by God in the Old Testament, why don't we follow all of them? I am told it is because Jesus fulfilled the law so it's no longer necessary. If that is true, why do we still revere the traditional Ten Commandments?

Why are we allowed to eat rare meat (Leviticus 19:26), live after committing adultery (Leviticus 20:10) and work on the Sabbath? Why do Christians pick and choose which laws of the Old Testament are still binding and which are not? Could it be because some laws of the Old Testament still appeal to them and others do not? Could it be that Christians, just like the rest of society, adopt moral laws using their own, their family's, and their culture's guidance instead of a supposedly absolute morality imposed upon them by a deity?

If Jesus fulfilled the law and made the Old Testament commandments unnecessary, then the traditional Ten Commandments are outdated. Jesus, in Matthew chapter 19, verses 18 and 19 said the commandments to follow are:

- ✓ Do not kill
- ✓ Do not commit adultery
- ✓ Do not steal
- ✓ Do not lie
- ✓ Honor your father and mother
- ✓ Love your neighbor as yourself

There aren't ten of them and he left out one of the greatest. Jesus said the greatest commandments were to love God with all your heart and your neighbor as yourself. The first could be considered a rendition of the commandment to have no other gods before Yahweh. The second is a rule of social behavior found in Leviticus 19:18, in which we are also told not to take revenge or hold a grudge against fellow countrymen. Jesus says these two are the greatest commandments, that "the whole law and the prophets depend on" them. (Matt 22:36-40) If we put them all together, we have only seven commandments according to Jesus.

Jesus didn't say to ignore any of God's other commandments. In fact, he said quite the opposite:

> Do not think that I have come to abolish the law or the prophets. I have come not to abolish but to fulfill. Amen, I say to you, until Heaven and earth pass away, not the smallest letter or the smallest part of a letter will pass from the law, until all things have taken place. (Matt 5:17-18)

If fulfill means to end, then Jesus contradicts himself. Heaven and Earth haven't passed away as far as I can tell, so all things haven't yet come to pass...so why are Christians daily ignoring the law of Yahweh? Because morals change; there is no absolute morality.

Do not kill. If that is one of God's absolutes, why do so many conservative Christians support the death penalty? If "do not kill" really means do not murder, it's not absolute after all. Murder is a relative term. When is killing murder? When is it an act of war? When is it justifiable? "Do not kill" either means no killing of any kind under any circumstance, or it is a situational, subjective commandment.

There is no absolute morality handed to us by a god. Our morals have developed and changed throughout the evolution of our species. I get my morals the same way Christians do. The big difference is that somewhere along the way, they were told that it is immoral to not believe in and worship their god. In that respect, no matter how good and moral a person I am, I will always be immoral in the eyes of a Christian.

I've been told that atheists and practitioners of other religions borrow moral codes from Christianity. Christianity, they say, brought morality to the world and we benefit from it while reviling it. We are unappreciative sycophants flailing against the very philosophy that supports us. This is untrue.

Christianity is not the originator of morality. Law is a reflection of each culture's morality. The codification of laws originated within the moral systems of human groups. The earliest known codification of laws was done by the King of Ur about 2100 BCE. Hammurabi codified a comprehensive set of laws during his reign in Babylon from 1795 to 1750 BCE. But even before laws were organized and written down, societies lived by their own moral codes. All cultures survive by adhering to codes of conduct. To claim that Christianity was, or even that the Hebrews were, the first to bring about a moral code for humanity is ludicrous and shows a terrible lack of historical understanding. Mankind created systems of morality and conduct on its own, long before the Hebrews adopted the warrior god Yahweh and long before pagan Jews created their own risen savior.

Chapter Ten

What's My Problem?

In some awful, strange, paradoxical way, atheists tend to take religion more seriously than the practitioners.
—Jonathon Miller (as quoted on the Internet)

Many Christians with whom I've spoken are genuinely concerned about my atheism. They seem to feel that if I only understood God, the Bible and Christianity the proper way, I'd come to believe in those things. At least one has offered to study the gospels with me, to answer my objections and explain to me where my misunderstanding occurred. I appreciate their feelings and their kindness and I understand their strong faith in what they believe. I've studied Christianity from an objective viewpoint and learned from Christians themselves enough to know that the explanations meant to convert me fall far short.

The quick answer to why I don't believe what they believe is because I'm a rationalist. The long answer is that, aside from simply not believing in gods, I find the Christian faith to be false and immoral so that, even were I to be a supernaturalist, I would not be Christian.

Rationalism

I am not a scholar or a philosopher; I'm an average person with an interest in the differences between believers and nonbelievers. I don't pretend that we will come to any agreement; I certainly don't expect others to accept my reasoning against their beliefs. I only want it understood and accepted that I, and most other atheists, have not dismissed Christianity without thorough consideration.

Rationalists claim reason, not subjective experience, authority or spiritual revelation, is the primary basis of knowledge. That is why I don't believe what others believe. I am unwilling to allow someone else to tell me what is true, to assume gods when the evidence doesn't support their existence, and to accept an answer because I feel I must have an answer when there isn't one to be had.

Science

I accept the scientific process as the best method we have for determining the nature of our reality. I understand that many people, not just Christians, are wary of science because it doesn't agree with their ideas regarding supernaturalism and the spiritual realm. Science doesn't delve into that realm because there is nothing there to be objectively studied. The evidence suggests it doesn't exist.

There is no conspiracy in the scientific community against the supernatural as Christians, astrologists and chakra practitioners are wont to claim. There is simply nothing there for science to deal with. If it can't be tested, measured, or authenticated, if its effects can't be reproduced, we can't know anything about it and it is, therefore, equal to nonexistent. I understand that many won't agree with that because they have accepted the existence of a supernatural realm that can only be verified through subjective experience and spiritual or authoritative revelation. As a rationalist, I do not accept those as evidence. They are, as far as I can discern, products of the psychology of humans; they are in your mind only. If they can't be objectively researched, we can never be sure of them and certainly can't claim any knowledge of them.

The scientific method is a valuable tool. It has brought us from the Dark Ages through the Enlightenment to this great age. I trust the scientific method; it has enabled us to objectively and rationally study our reality. Too few people know what the scientific method is. In the scientific community, claims are based on evidence; theories are tested and peer-reviewed. People suspicious of the scientific method often point to arguments and disagreements among scientists as evidence that scientific claims, such as evolution, aren't valid. "Scientists can't even agree on it," they say, "so how are we supposed to believe it's true."

If we look closely at the scientific community, however, what we find is a system of checks and balances that allows us to evaluate theories and findings and reasonably accept conclusions. Scientists disagree; that's the beauty of the search for reality. There is no science dogma to which scientists must adhere. New findings are subject to peer review and unbiased testing. Scientists do disagree on some aspects of evolutionary theories such as how it occurred, but the vast majority of scientists agree that evolution explains our human origins.

Christians also claim that scientists are biased against the supernatural and God, and try very hard to ignore any evidence that might lead to anything but a naturalistic conclusion. Just imagine if a scientist could come up with objective evidence for the supernatural. If anyone could offer repeatable, testable evidence that proved ESP, chakras, angels, the effectiveness of prayer, or God, he'd be a celebrity. He wouldn't be ridiculed or banished from the scientific community if his theory had objective, testable evidence to back it up. But no such evidence exists.

Evolution

Creationists make it sound as though a 'theory' is something you dreamt up after being drunk all night.

—Isaac Asimov

I accept the facts that show us our evolutionary heritage. The subject of evolution is a big one with Christians. Many accept the facts and simply attach evolution to their god's plan but there are still those, the loudest it seems, who deny the facts, claim evolution is "just a theory," a lie, and that creation as told by the Bible is the truth. I will not discuss the various evolutionary theories here; hundreds of books are available to anyone who wants to learn about them. I wanted to include evolution here for a particular reason.

I don't *believe in* evolution. I am not an *evolutionist*. Phrasing it that way is a blatant attempt on the part of many Christians to make acceptance of the facts of evolution into a faith so that they might claim it is no different than what they do when they choose Christianity. That is a lie and a rationalization made for the express purpose of avoiding the fact that they have no evidence to support their view that a god created the world and humans, as described in the Bible. There is no

evidence for Creationism. Creationism, therefore, is something that ne-
cessitates a belief. You must *believe in* Creationism because it is not
based on facts.

I don't *believe in* evolution; I don't have to. I simply accept the
facts that I have seen and read about. The difference between a rationalist and a Creationist is evident in this debate. The Creationist already
knows what is true for him—an authority has given him his truth in the
Bible. All the facts must support that truth. No facts that dispute it will
be accepted; worse, facts can be created, made up, *fabricated* as long as
they support his truth.

The rationalist, on the other hand, is free to accept facts as they
are. He creates a theory based on those facts. A scientific theory
doesn't mean a guess, an assumption, or a made-up story. A scientific theory is an explanation based on supporting facts. The great
thing about science is that theories change. When new facts are discovered that contradict long-held theories, they aren't ignored, they
aren't banned, they aren't called heresy or changed to fit the theory;
they *change the theory*. Rationalists are free to accept new ideas; we
have no authority that tells us what is true. Creationists find facts to
fit their truth. Rationalists discover the truth that fits the facts. One
position is noble, the other is not. One is honest, the other is not. One is
truth, the other, a lie.

Truth
There aren't any versions of the truth.
  —Dr. Ian Malcolm in *Jurassic Park II: The Lost World*
                                         (Universal, 1997)

What is truth? Some people talk about Truth, with a capital T, as if
it is an ultimate idea that transcends all life and reality. When I say
truth, I'm talking about plain, simple, factual truth. Not a truth for me,
different from your truth; and not an ultimate, great truth. I'm talking
about *the* truth; the only one.

I've heard it said that one person's truth is another's lie. This is
not the kind of truth I'm looking for. Let's say that Person A believes the moon is made of green cheese. Person B believes the
moon is made of ham. If every person holds his own truth, then
both of these persons are correct. But, neither is correct. The truth
is that the moon is a rock. That truth will never change and it

doesn't matter what people believe about the moon, or how many people believe it, there is a truth with regard to it that can be discovered.

I want the truth. I don't want to believe in something. If there isn't an answer to a question, like, how did life on Earth arise, then I will have to wait until there is, or die without it because I would rather be without an answer than believe in something that may not be the truth.

In the final chapter of *Does God Exist?* (Prometheus, 1993), a debate between J.P. Moreland and Kai Nelson, Peter Kreeft discusses "The Choice of a Lifetime," or how to decide what position you will take after reading the debate and discussions pertaining to it. He starts out fine in highlighting the advice that we should be honest with ourselves and we must look at all evidence on both sides. But from there he digresses into a disgusting display of emotionalism and the threat of Pascal's Wager. We should look at lives, he says, to determine the truth; and people's lives have been changed for the better with Christianity. We should try living our lives as if we were Christians and then as if we were nonbelievers and see which one is more satisfying, as if this will lead us to the truth. Finally, he speaks of the possibilities: either God exists or he doesn't and we either believe in him or we don't, and only the one combination of those choices (he exists and we believe) will earn us "the infinite prize of eternal life." "Faith," he says, "is a 'no-lose' bet and atheism is a 'no-win' bet."

This is how we should determine truth? We imagine a frightful scenario of eternal torture versus a paradise and then see what feels good or hedge our bets? This is why Christianity is akin to snake-oil to me, and its apologists fear-mongers. I don't determine what is true by how I feel. I want the facts.

Why I am not a Christian

Certainly my rationalist view affects the manner in which I interpret and understand theism. It is because I am a rationalist that I am atheist. But what is it that makes me think I would not be Christian even were I to accept a supernatural realm? There are many tenets of the Christian faith that, when viewed objectively, show it to be false and immoral. Much of Christianity only makes sense when viewed historically as layer upon layer of apologetics were created to explain discrepancies and contradictions.

The omni god and free will

Epicurus said,

> Either God wants to abolish evil, and cannot; or he can, but
> does not want to...If he wants to, but cannot, he is impotent. If
> he can, but does not want to, he is wicked... If, as they say, God
> can abolish evil, and God really wants to do it, why is there evil
> in the world?

When you discuss the Christian god with Christians, you begin to
get a picture of it and its attributes. God is omnipotent, omnipresent,
omniscient and omni-benevolent. In other words, he is all powerful,
everywhere, all knowing and all good. God gave us something called
free will. Free will is supposed to explain why the world is in the state
it is while there is an omni God at the helm. Free will is the excuse
Christians invented for God's ineptness and inattention.

The Christian god can not possibly exist. Christians have unwit-
tingly defined their god into nonexistence—he has disappeared in a
puff of illogic. No entity can have all the omni attributes and offer free
will at the same time.

God can't be all powerful; he can't do absolutely anything; he is
limited. Christians say, for instance, that he can't do something that is
logically impossible, such as create a rock so big he can't lift it himself,
or create a square circle. Christians get exasperated when atheists and
skeptics play logic games like that with them. They think we're being
facetious, but we're just pointing out that no entity can be all
powerful. There is no conceivable way for God to be omnipotent. He is
limited by logic, and any limit imposed on him makes him less than all
powerful.

God is supposed to be all good and can't do anything that is not
good. Therefore, he is again limited. I've been told that God can't
kill himself or cease to exist. There are plenty of things that God
can't do.

In the Bible, God is certainly not described as omnipotent. He
couldn't help Judah defeat a certain population because they had iron
chariots (Judges 1:19). That's silly, of course, to think that a god could
be bested by iron chariots, but it's in the Bible.

Jesus is God, I'm told, and yet, in his home town, he couldn't work
any miracles because the people there didn't believe in him (Matt

13:57-58). That always made me wonder...he wasn't powerful enough to overcome disbelief. Only people who already believed in him would believe in him.

Christians sometimes explain God's power problem by redefining the word "all" to mean "all within his capability." Using that definition, I, too am all powerful because I can do everything within my capability. God can't do anything he wants to do. He is bound by the rules of logic (and steel) and by his own good nature. Therefore, he is not all powerful. He is more powerful than man, I'll give you that. He's just not omnipotent.

God is not omniscient. The Bible is clear on that point. In Genesis, God didn't know where Adam was or that he'd eaten from the forbidden fruit (Gen 3:9-11). He didn't know why Eve ate the fruit and offered it to Adam (Gen 3: 13). And he didn't know what happened to Abel (Gen 4:9). God can't be omniscient if mankind has free will. If we truly have choices to make, God can't know what we will choose before we choose it. If God knows what we will do, our future is already told. His prior knowledge eliminates our freedom of choice, making it an illusion.

Christians tell me that God knows everything there is to know as it happens; this wouldn't include the future. But then, they also tell me that God knew that man would rebel and he would have to send himself down as Jesus to die on the cross for our salvation—he knew all that from the beginning of time. Others tell me that we have complete free will, but God just knows the choices we will make ahead of time. I'm confused. Does God know everything, including the future? Or does God only know the past and present? It's really very simple. I don't know why Christian doctrine is always making things difficult: either we truly have free will and God is not omniscient, or God is omniscient and the future is already set—we can't do anything to change it.

God is not omni-benevolent. Instead of disciplining with love as a human parent strives to do, the Christian god punishes people viciously. He drowned all humans including small children in a worldwide flood (Gen 6:17). He caused the Earth to swallow people up (Num16: 32-33), and tortured complainers by sending serpents to bite them (Num 21:6). An all-good being wouldn't be able to punish anyone in this manner. He commanded people to murder others (Num 31) and is vengeful (Deut 32:35). God allows evil in the world. He doesn't stop the murderer or rapist from his designs against innocent humans. Christians say that is because God gave us free will. That's fine. But it shows that God can't be all good. He could be good; just not all good. No omnibenevolent creature could allow evil to flourish when he is powerful enough to stop it; and he certainly wouldn't engage in evil acts himself.

If God is omnipotent and has the desire for all mankind to be saved, all mankind would be saved. Anything an all-powerful God wants, he gets; because he's all powerful. I'm told that this doesn't happen, that all men aren't saved, because there is something else that God wants. He wants us to have free will to choose him or reject him. I don't think it says that anywhere in the Bible. It says, "All things are possible for God," (Mark 10:27) and that God is "not wishing that any should perish but that all should come to repentance." (2Peter 3:9) Nowhere does it say, "…but more than this, God wants you to have the free will to turn away from him and not be saved." It's just not there. Free will is something that Christians made up to explain inconsistencies in their religion.

There are some Christians who don't believe in free will. They find plenty of support for their position in the Bible: "The Lord brings to naught the plans of nations; he foils the designs of peoples. But the plan of the Lord stands forever; the design of his heart, through all generations." (Psalm 33:9-11) "Our God is in Heaven; whatever he wills, he does." (Psalm 15:3) "In the beginning I foretell the outcome; in advance, things not yet done. I say that my plan shall stand, I accomplish my every purpose." (Isaiah 46:10)

It is very clear by those verses that God has a plan and nothing we do can change it. Whatever God wills, is done. That means that God wills some people to be Christian just as he has willed that I should be atheist. He wills that some will be homosexual and some heterosexual. He wills that some should be slaughtered in war, maimed, raped, or tortured and he wills that others should die peacefully. God is in control, not us. Nothing has gone wrong with this world that God has not willed. The fall of man, sin, evil, Satan, murder—it's all God's will. Christians have no right to judge what God has willed.

As Epicurus noted, if God is in charge, there is no free will. If God is all good, there can be no evil. If God wanted to stop evil and had the power to do so, he would. He's either powerless to act, making him useless, or he's vile and mean. Or, maybe, he's just fiction.

The Trinity

The Trinity is a very strange concept but it had to be invented. Some early Christians believed that Jesus was God. In order for the tribulation on the cross to make sense, he had to be a man, too, because gods can't suffer and die. The only answer was that Jesus was God and man—fully God and fully man at the same time. That is, of course, impossible and illogical but it must be believed if Christianity is to make any sense at all.

Strangely enough in the Old Testament it is written that, "God is not man that he should speak falsely, nor human, that he should change his mind." (Num 23:19) Nonetheless, early Christians, for whatever reason, ignored the scripture and determined that God was, indeed, man, at least for a little while. Obviously man has a problem with telling the truth. As Paul said, "...every human being is a liar..." (Rom 3: 10) Why we are expected to believe anything Paul said after that is one of my big questions. How are we are supposed to believe Jesus' words as well, considering that he was fully man? Knowing God's penchant for sending lying spirits to the mouths of prophets (1Kings 22:23), it is well within reason to distrust the entire story.

The Trinity divides God into three parts: the Father, the Son and the Holy Spirit. They are three separate entities but they are each God at the same time. They are one and three and impossible to believe. If God can be three and one, I fail to see the problem with his creating a rock so big he can't lift it. If he must stay within the realm of logic, what is he doing mixed up with the Trinity?

God sent himself down to become a man. He was still himself, but he called himself Jesus and walked the Earth, while he was still in Heaven and called himself the Father. He had himself tortured and killed (though he couldn't die because he was God) and buried. He rose again, though he was already alive. He ascended into Heaven where he had been the whole time.

Remember that nonsense poem we recited in school?

> One fine day in the middle of the night
> Two dead men got up to fight
> Back to back they faced each other
> Drew their swords and shot each other

That's the Trinity for you. It makes no sense.

The family thing

One of my biggest questions regarding Jesus involves his miraculous birth. While it is extremely difficult to believe the mythical element of virgin conception—of the Holy Spirit, being God, actually impregnating a woman—that's not the problem. My confusion arose when I read about Jesus as a grown man and his parents' and the townspeople's reaction to him.

In the beginning, Mary was approached by an angel who told her she would conceive a child by a holy spirit (meaning God, the Father, and the son Jesus, too...Jesus is his own father!). This angel said to Mary of Jesus, "He will be great and will be called Son of the Most High, and the Lord God will give him the throne of David his father..." (Luke 1:32) An angel visited Joseph, Mary's fiancé, too, because he was thinking of breaking the engagement. The angel told him that Jesus would "...save his people from their sins." (Matt. 1: 21)

Jesus was born in a manger and three wise men from the East headed over to pay him homage. His birth was apparently a glorious and renowned thing. But...for some reason it was all forgotten. The people in the town of Nazareth didn't think Jesus was anything special. I suppose I can buy the theory that Mary and Joseph didn't tell anyone about the relationship between their son and God (that he was Jesus' real father) and that Jesus was the promised Messiah. You'd think after all the fuss with Herod killing baby boys, people would have been on the look out for a Messiah of about the right age who could have escaped the massacre. When Jesus showed up, they didn't find him special; no one seemed to remember his family's secret flight out of the country during Herod's slaughter. I can accept the theory that they didn't recognize him because God had a plan; God blinded them to the truth. But what I can't believe is that Jesus' own mother and brothers didn't know who he was.

Jesus' brothers, according to John, didn't believe in him. (John 7:5) How could that be? How could they have been raised with the son of God/God himself and not known it? Why would Jesus' relatives claim he was insane? (Mark 3: 21)

Worse is the behavior of his mother and father. They accidentally left him behind in Jerusalem and went back to find him in the temple teaching. "When his parents saw him they were astonished." (Luke 2: 48) Why? Didn't they remember he was the son of God/God? Jesus explained to them that it was natural for them to find him in his father's house, but "they did not understand what he said to them." (Luke 2:50) How can that be? How can two people experience a miracle in their lives, take an adventurous sojourn into Egypt to rescue the savior of mankind from Herod (Matt 2:13-14) and forget all about it? It isn't possible. If God blinded Jesus' parents to the truth, why did he bother sending the messenger angels? Why didn't he just wait until Mary was married to have sex with her? Then no one would have suspected anything for him to have to cover up. It just doesn't make sense.

The problem was evidently caused by a later insertion of a virgin birth story and a parallel to Moses' escape from Pharaoh into the narrative. That's what happens when you create and expand myths; they become convoluted and nonsensical.

The problem at home

When Jesus went home to Nazareth he couldn't work miracles there because the people didn't believe in him. According to Matthew, "Jesus said to them, 'A prophet is not without honor except in his native place and in his own house.' And he did not work many mighty deeds there because of their lack of faith." (Matt 13: 57-58) Why do you suppose people in a person's home town don't believe he is anything special? Could it be because they know him? Maybe they knew he wasn't who he claimed to be. Why would their lack of belief have anything to do with Jesus' ability to perform miracles? If you had to believe Jesus could do miracles before he could do them, how do we know the stories of the miracles aren't just due to imagination and desire to believe? Wouldn't Jesus have wanted to perform miracles for people who didn't believe in him so they could be saved? Being that he was God, he should have been able to make anything he wanted to happen easily come about.

Some Christians have told me that it is precisely this sort of problem in the gospels that can be used as evidence of their validity. Because the gospels do not always show Jesus in a good light and perfect, they must have been written by people trying hard to be objective. If everything was perfect about Jesus, about the Bible—if the gospel narratives had no contradictions—that would cause them to suspect something was amiss. As they are, they show the work of honest men.

That is one way to look at it, I suppose, but there is another explanation. If you accept that the stories of Jesus' life began orally and weren't written down at the same time, you can imagine the building of the myth. Mark is acknowledged to have been written first in about 70 CE with the rest through about 110 CE when John was composed. Reading the Gospels in chronological order—Mark, Matthew, Luke, then John—you see the building of the cult of Jesus, from basic information about his teachings to miraculous conception and full-fledged godhood. When people retell and rewrite stories for their own audiences, elements are added and changed causing conflicts and errors in the manuscripts. That is why the gospel stories are contradictory and grow more and more mythical with the years.

As to the character of Jesus, we may never know in what manner the authors of the original stories meant their works to be interpreted. If we consider, however, that early followers of the cult may not have accepted Jesus as a historical figure, but as symbolic, or even as a mere man, the fact that he wasn't presented as a perfect god makes sense.

The truth about the parables

Timothy said that God, our savior, "wills everyone to be saved and come to knowledge of the truth." (1Tim 2:4) Did Jesus/God want people to be saved? The disciples asked Jesus why he taught in parables and he said, "...so that they may look and see but not perceive, and hear and listen but not understand, in order that they may not be converted and be forgiven." (Mark 4: 12) God contradicts himself. He does and he doesn't want everyone to be saved.

According to the Bible, many people didn't believe Jesus' teachings so Isaiah's prophecy could come true: "He blinded their eyes and hardened their heart, so that they might not see with their eyes and understand with their heart and be converted and I would heal them." (John 12:40) So I have to wonder which is correct. Does God want everyone saved or not? If he wants everyone saved, why would he blind eyes and harden hearts to prevent it?

❧❧❧❧

These are just some of the questions and issues I have about the story of Jesus and Christianity. I am sure apologists have answers to all of my problems; they can smooth away any contradictions and make sense of atrocities. I have little doubt I've heard the excuses before. None of them are convincing to me. I think perhaps we should just agree to disagree.

Chapter Eleven

But, What Do I Really Think?

With or without religion, good people can behave well and bad people can do evil; but for good people to do evil—that takes religion.

—Steven Weinberg (as quoted on the Internet)

Literalist Christianity is an immoral lie. I realize that opinion may be shocking to most people. The majority of the world has been deceived into believing they are educated about Christianity, its precepts, its moral goodness, its historical base, and its history. Most Christians have never read the Bible. Most Christians have never studied history as told by the opposition or by true historians. Most Christians don't even go to church. Those that do simply accept what their pastor tells them and what they read in books written for the express purpose of defending the Christian lie. Most Christians will continue to be deceived because instead of truth, they want comfort. The comfortable path is generally the path you're already on. Change isn't something humans enjoy. Most of us will only accept it when it is forced on us.

Searching for truth is an active pursuit but it isn't an easy one. It takes diligence and discipline. It takes a commitment to put aside one's longings and emotions for objectivity. It takes an understanding of what bias is, how it invades our thinking and how to purge ourselves of it. To add to that, the truth about our reality isn't an easy one and humans aren't very big on difficulty. We generally take the rutted path, or remain on the road we find ourselves walking along.

I started my educational journey through the precepts and history of Christianity with a reading of the Bible. It was after this reading that I came to the firm conclusion that Christianity was immoral and even if it were true, I would not be able to worship its god.

The problem with religion is that it is taught to us as something sacred. It is given to us as holy and above question and reproach. To question the tenets of your religion is equal to questioning God himself and is sinful. We elevate our religious precepts and symbols to a place where they can not be touched; we put them in a separate place even in our minds so that we don't allow our reason to probe them. We do this because religion is all about what we don't know but must believe. If we could dissect the dogma and show it to be true, belief and faith would be unnecessary. We know we can't do that; we know that our religions are not factual. But to face that truth—to bring it to the fore of our consciousness—would destroy our faith. So we push it back, deep into a place that reason isn't allowed to penetrate. We make religion sacred because it can't survive skeptical discourse.

The Bible

Evidence against the validity of the Bible abounds. One of the most fervent claims of Christians is that the Bible is historically accurate. I used to counter this claim with the obvious conclusion that just because the Bible is historically accurate in some spots doesn't make its mythical claims any less fallacious; and that was true. However, with more investigation I found that modern archeological evidence destroys the historicity of the Bible. The Bible is, after all, the exaggerated claims of a backward and oppressed people.

After reading the Bible, I had to wonder why it is so revered in our society. How could such a book filled with inaccuracies, atrocities, and mythology be touted as truth? Why do people simply accept traditional explanations and continue teaching them to generation after generation without bothering to question what they're doing? How many people have actually read the entire Bible?

People are comforted by ritual and tradition; they use symbols to make their spiritual beliefs meaningful. The Bible is one symbol; they like the feel of it, the way its paperback cover lays back and its delicate pages rustle when turned. It's a heavy, well-made book that fits nicely in the crook of an arm. People claim the Bible is special; they feel special holding it, flipping through it, and reading snippets of it here and there. When something is established in ritual, people do it without thinking. The majority reads and reveres the Bible because they're taught to, not because it has any truth in it.

Hell and a loving god

The concept of Hell is immoral. Many Christians have managed to distance themselves from the idea because they agree that eternal punishment is not in line with a loving and just god. Modern mainstream Christianity seems to be of the opinion that God equals goodness and love. This all sounds acceptable and is probably what keeps mainstream Christianity alive.

Fundamentalist, conservative Christianity may continue its claim that God is love, but it doesn't hide its acceptance of God as vengeful and cruel in its perceptions of the Rapture, when the blood of the wicked will fill the streets, and Hell, where the screams of tortured souls will be pleasing to the ears of the saved. Normal, well-balanced, loving people don't accept those ideas as well they should not—they are immoral.

Looking at Hell from the literalist perspective we see an entity creating an imperfect being and then punishing it for its failings. At worst, the punishment is an eternal torture and at best, simply the absence of the presence of the creator. Mainstream Christianity has struggled with the problem of Hell as a place of torture. How does Love create a place of torment and punish people eternally there for crimes committed in this very short lifetime? While we can give some credence to the idea of punishing extremely bad behavior for some length of time, the condemnation of nonbelief and mistaken belief seems unnecessarily cruel. How is it the fault of the Muslim for believing Islam when he was born and raised to believe it? How can a just god punish him for it? How can a just and loving god punish an agnostic for honestly claiming that he feels he can't know whether or not a god exists?

One answer I have received from Christians is not helpful: God doesn't send us to Hell, they say, we send ourselves there by denying God. But, the Christian god is said to have created Hell; and he created humans with an imperfect nature—if we were created perfect, there would have been no fall, no matter how much temptation God placed in the garden. Perfect creatures don't make imperfect choices. How can sin be the fault of the imperfect creation? God creates sinful beings and then punishes them for the way he created them.

It is God who must be imperfect, for a perfect god could only create perfect creatures. A perfectly loving god could only love those creatures. God must be imperfect (not hard to believe after a good reading of the Bible) and he punishes mankind for his own sin.

Some Christians believe that their god creates some humans knowing they will go to Hell; I've heard that some humans are created for the express purpose of going to Hell. Proverbs 16:4 says, "The Lord has made everything for his own ends, even the wicked for the evil day." This doesn't sound like the Christian concept of a loving god to me at all.

One Christian told me that all people, even Muslims in the Middle East, know that Jesus is our savior and the only reason they don't consciously seek this truth is their own sinful natures. So, a Muslim born into and raised in Islam is inherently at fault for not accepting the truth he knows, that Jesus is the savior, and shunning Islam. Talk about elitism!

Another answer is that no one knows who will be in Hell and who will not. Some Christians say that they have no doubt there will be atheists in Heaven. Some believe that Hell may be only temporary. I appreciate that these people are honest about their aversion to the concept of eternal torment for humans but I don't think their ideas are Biblical. Jesus very clearly said that all those who don't believe in him were condemned and that hell is an eternal punishment. (Matt. 25:46; Mark 16:16; John 3:18)

Many people claim that Hell is not Biblical at all. They say that Hell is a modern concept added to the Church in later days. The condemnation of Jesus, then, must mean something else. And what of Revelation and its bizarre story of a vengeful god destroying the wicked in a second coming? Either believe the entire Bible, or don't believe any of it. Why pick and choose? By what criteria do we believe some of it true and the rest false? If it isn't all true, is it the word of a god? And if not, why believe any of it?

I've heard others say that hell isn't permanent; that the punishment will fit the crime and some even believe that eventually every human soul will be in Heaven. I, personally, think they're making all of that up to make an immoral deity into something palatable to modern theism.

Heaven

What will Heaven be like? Will everyone be good in Heaven? Some Christians have told me that living in Heaven, in the presence of God who is pure love and goodness, humans will no longer sin. But Adam and Eve lived in God's presence and they still sinned. Some say that in Heaven, we'll have free will just as we do now. People who do bad things will be cast out of Heaven immediately. If humans can be good all the time in Heaven, or bad people will be cast out, why didn't God create us in Heaven to begin with—why the passion play?

The purpose of the Earth creation, some have said, is a test. Our loyalty is being tested, our faith and belief, our obedience. Why? Why can't we know now that God exists; why can't we live in his presence and have a chance to know him and love him? Why do we have to just believe that he exists because other people tell us he does? Why would an all-knowing deity need a test?

Such a test, in the opinion of many, is unfair but I am told that God, as usual, has his reasons and I am always assured that his reasons are good ones. Because he is God and god is defined as good, anything he decides is good, whether I think so or not.

Heaven just doesn't make sense. If we get tested and only the good people get to go to Heaven, why didn't God just create only those good people? If only the people who believe in God by faith without evidence get in, why didn't he just create people like that in the first place?

Others have told me that Earth is like a training ground. An oak begins as an acorn, they say. This life isn't a test, it's our infancy and here we must learn to trust in God. Right...those of us who fail to learn get tossed into the flaming abyss. It always boils down to Heaven as a reward, a prize to be won, not by using our brains, but by turning away from all that our reason tells us is true and instead, believing in something nonsensical and contradictory. I can handle that. I can see that brownie points could be awarded to people who use faith. But that doesn't make the situation moral.

The fall of man

The fall of man, as described in the Bible, makes no sense. It goes pretty much like this: God creates Adam and Eve and they are perfect (or simply good, depending on the apologist). God sets them in a garden where he also plants two trees, the tree of knowledge of good and evil and the tree of life. God only mentions the first tree to A&E and tells them not to eat any of the fruit; if they do, they'll die. Along comes a serpent, wily and cunning. Who let him into the garden? Where did God disappear to? The serpent tempts Eve. Eve, we must remember, is innocent; she hasn't eaten from the tree of knowledge of good and evil yet, so she obviously doesn't have any knowledge about them. Eve is perfect and living in the presence of the divine and holy god but, for some odd reason she is tempted by the serpent. The serpent claims that God is a liar; he says, "No, God knows well that the moment you eat of it your eyes will be opened and you will be like gods who know what is good and what is bad." (Gen 3:5) So, she eats the fruit and gives some to Adam.

The problems with this story are enough to cause a person some pause. Why did God allow his creatures to be tempted in such a manner? Why did he put the tree in the garden at all? Many Christians tell me that it was all part of the plan, that God knew what would happen. But, that would be despicable. To create beings that you know will disobey you if you plant the right temptations in their home and then to punish them and all their progeny for it is not the behavior of a just and loving father.

Even worse, the serpent told the truth! Adam and Eve did not die when they ate the fruit as God said they would. Many Christians have tried to claim that God didn't mean they were going to die right then, he meant that they were immortal until they ate the fruit and then God cast them out and let them succumb to physical death later. This is not possible, however, if you believe the Bible. The scripture clearly shows that after A&E ate the fruit of the first tree, God was quick to hustle them out of the garden "lest they should eat of the tree of life and live forever." (Gen 3:22) Adam and Eve were not immortal to begin with. God said they'd die the day they ate the fruit. God lied. The serpent told the truth.

I suppose it is possible, as I've been told by one Christian, that God was letting A&E eat from the tree of life to get their daily dose of immortality and only stopped them from doing so after they figured out good and evil. We can't have immortal beings knowing good and evil—like gods. Unfortunately, the Bible doesn't say anything like that.

Why did God lie? If he wanted a fallen, sinful man, why didn't he just make him that way? Why, instead, go to all the trouble to make mankind's sinful nature look like man's fault? Something is very fishy there.

To fix the lie problem some Christians tell me that God didn't mean "die physically," but that Adam and Eve would "die spiritually." The Bible doesn't say that. It says nothing about the spirit or spiritual death; it says Adam will die. In trying to argue for a spiritual death, Christians are adding their own words and ideas to God's in order to force some sense out of the story. That is a sin according to Revelation, which says,

> I warn everyone who hears the prophetic words in this book: If anyone adds to them, God will add to him the plagues described in this book, and if anyone takes away from the words in this prophetic book, God will take away his share in the tree of life and in the holy city described in this book. (Rev. 22:18)

I think the author is only referring to his particular book, Revelation, which is, in my opinion, the ravings of a lunatic but some Christians tell me the warning refers to the entire Bible. If that is true, how can they claim that the word "spiritually" should be added to Genesis 2:17 and 3:3? Why does it never occur to these Christians that maybe it's just an imperfect story written by humans thousands of years ago?

Christians also claim that with the fall, mankind invited sin into the world. Paul says in Romans 5, verse 12, "Therefore, just as through one person sin entered the world, and through sin, death, and thus death came to all, inasmuch as all sinned..." However, God doesn't say anything about that in Genesis. According to the Bible, the curse of the fall had nothing to do with mankind suddenly having a sinful nature. Here is the punishment man received for his disobedience:

To the woman:
✓ intensified pangs of childbearing
✓ urge for your husband; he'll be your master

To the man:
✓ the ground is cursed; you'll have to work hard to get food from it

That's it. That's the sum total of the curse on Adam and Eve, nothing about mankind now being filled with sin. Strangely enough, God had already put Adam in the garden in the first place to "cultivate and care for it." (Gen 2:15) I guess the ground in Eden was easier to work than the cursed ground outside it after the eviction. The way I see it, early Christians added the concept of sin to the Genesis story and in truth, the curse wasn't much of one.

All through the Bible, God sets people up only to punish them, tortures and murders humans unnecessarily (assuming you haven't bought into the it's-man's-own-fault-he's-wicked excuse the god of the Bible would have you believe), and wreaks havoc wherever he can. And yet, we are supposed to believe God equals love and justice. Something just isn't right with this story.

The ultimate blood sacrifice

In the Old Testament, Yahweh was pleased with the smell of burning animal flesh (Gen. 8:21; Exod. 29:18, 25, 41; Lev. 1:13, 17; Num. 15:7, etc.). I have been told that later in time a sacrifice was again necessary for the sins of mankind. No ordinary sacrifice would do this time. This time, it would be one final, huge sacrifice: God would send himself down to Earth as his own son/self and offer himself up as a savior. This last sacrifice was supposed to be the greatest and most meaningful of all but, it doesn't make any sense.

Why does the Christian god punish innocent people for others' crimes, as he did with Adam's progeny (Rom. 5:12) and King David's son (2Sam 12:14), and forgive others' crimes by punishing an innocent man/god, Jesus? Where is the justice in this system? How could we have possibly come up with the fairness of our justice system if we were instilled with Yahweh's manner of justice? It is an abhorrent and irreconcilably unfair system. Under any normal circumstances a Christian would agree but, because this is his god we're talking about, he defends it as somehow meaningful, good and just. Until Christians can explain to me how it is meaningful, good and just that an innocent person must pay for someone else's sins, we will have to be at odds.

Another problem with Jesus' sacrifice is that there doesn't seem to be one. What exactly was the great sacrifice? Jesus spent a few hours on a cross and died; but he is God! After he died, he got to live again and, better yet, go back to Heaven. What was so great about the short time on the cross?

I've been told that the sacrifice was in his taking all of our sins onto himself. But, again, he is supposed to be God. I don't see how an omnipresent and omnipotent god could have a problem with taking on all of humanity's sins, considering he's everywhere already and all-powerful, and considering it was his decision to inflict the sin in the first place. "It's because God is pure goodness," one Christian told me. "It is excruciatingly painful for him to abide sin, much less possess it himself." If this is true, how is it that God murdered the first-born of Egypt or the poor guy who steadied the "ark of the covenant" to keep it from falling (2Sam 6:6-7)? How is it that a purely good being engages in such cruelty, especially if it is painful to him? "Because he loves us," is the answer. It sounds like grasping at excuses to defend the indefensible to me.

※❂※❂※

My position with regard to Christianity is a harsh one. I believe it is a lie and an immoral one at that; but I know that Christians are not immoral people, in general. As with people of any other religion or philosophy, there are good and bad. One of the biggest problems I have with Christianity is that it can so easily be used for bad people to justify their hatred, intolerance, and vile acts against others.

When we look at the history of Christianity, we imagine Christians must be ashamed but, for some reason, they aren't. The Inquisition, the Crusades, the witch trials and burnings, the support of slavery in the southern United States, all are explained away as the acts of people who were not true Christians. But the hateful people who carried out these horrors were good Christians who believed they were following the word of God, the Bible, and they were. For every evil act and bigoted attitude expressed by man, a supporting scripture can be found.

How do Christians respond to that? "Don't blame God," they say. "It's not the fault of God's word, but of fallible mankind." I don't buy it. God himself (or a wise prophet) once said:

> By their fruits you will know them. Do people pick grapes
> from thornbushes, or figs from thistles? Just so, every good tree

bears good fruit, and a rotten tree bears bad fruit. A good tree
cannot bear bad fruit, nor can a rotten tree bear good fruit. (Matt
7:16-18)

If the Bible were truly the word of an all-loving, supreme, being
there would be nothing in it that could remotely be misconstrued and
used for evil purposes. No omnipotent deity could create such a horrible, misunderstood book without meaning to. Either the Christian god
is as evil as his book, or he didn't inspire the book, or...he doesn't exist
at all.

Chapter Twelve

The Voice of the Collective

I don't think of Christianity as a cult. Cult is a funny term, after all; it has many definitions and its usage may be determined by the user's feelings more than any truth in his claim. Originally cult meant, basically, religion; there was no negative connotation. Today, the most negative view of cults is of small, radical groups of people "brainwashed" into following a charismatic leader, often into some type of violence. Brainwashed is another funny term; it really just means heavily indoctrinated under significant pressure to conform.

But the word cult can just mean any group of people following a charismatic leader. Its members are indoctrinated into the beliefs of the group and those beliefs are interpreted and taught either by an individual leader, a group of leaders, an organization of leadership, or a combination of all three.

In the opinion of some Christian groups, a cult is a breakaway sect of Christianity itself that doesn't follow the mainstream. Their definition is laughable. A cult, they say, is a group of people who claim to be Christian, but embrace a doctrine (taught by an individual, group or organization) that denies one or more of the core doctrines of Christianity as taught by the Bible. It just seems to me that you could label Christianity as coming out of Judaism and denying one or more of the core doctrines of Judaism. Then you could describe Protestantism as a cult originating out of Catholicism and from there every new sect of Christianity could be said to be a cult. It's as if what they are saying, without hearing themselves, is that any group newer than their group is a cult.

The major sects that Christians seem to point their fingers at and label as cults are the Jehovah's Witnesses and Mormons. These two groups claim to be Christian while denying core doctrines such as the Trinity or the deity of Jesus; and of course, they each claim to be the One True Faith. "Cult!" cries the Biblical Christian who actually has the correct doctrine and belongs to the real One True Faith.

Christianity, as a whole, isn't necessarily a cult; it's too divided and broad. But, each sect, each denomination, each home church is its own little cult appendage, a fresh branch that will one day be able to point the finger at the newbies and cry, "Cult!" Christianity can be said to be a cult because it has many of the traits we associate with cults.

What makes a cult? In general, a cult is considered to be a group of people devoted to a charismatic leader. Cults employ manipulation to persuade and control members. Some of the forms of manipulation are: isolation from friends and family; pressure to conform to the group doctrine; information censorship and management; suspension of individuality and critical thinking; and promotion of dependence on the group. Cult groups might also physically debilitate people using drugs, fasting, marathon praying, sleep deprivation etc. to enhance the potency of their other methods in controlling members.

Cults, like any other group type, range from the extreme, like the Christian doomsday cult of Jim Jones, to the moderate sects of mainstream religions. People don't generally call Christianity a cult simply because it has become widespread, accepted, and it's not considered dangerous.

Still, Christianity is much like a cult. It is based on the charismatic leadership of Jesus as interpreted by the charismatic leaders of the individual churches. Christianity calls people to be reborn into new beings and to surround themselves with other Christians; new Christians, especially, are often told to be wary of non-Christians who might lead them away from their tenuous, newfound faith. There is much pressure from other Christians to conform to the standard doctrinal interpretations of the sect. Information is often withheld regarding responsibilities and practices until a new Christian is further indoctrinated into the faith. Afterward, reliance on scripture, as interpreted by the sect, is paramount and all other data is considered "worldly" and of Satan. While even the most evangelical adherents will deny it, critical thinking and individuality are to be set aside. Total reliance on the doctrine of the sect and an ethereal holy spirit is promoted and expected.

Christianity appears very much like a mild, culturally-acceptable cult. But because of the negative connotations of the term, a better description might be a Collective. The Collective of Christianity is broad and varied. There are many pockets containing different sorts of people. It is difficult to talk about the Collective as a whole and yet, all its members share in it. Those on the outer rim of the Collective don't bear as many of the Collective markings as those toward the inner circle. In the inner circle are the evangelicals and Biblical literalists. As you travel outward, adherents become more and more liberal, accepting less and less a literalist interpretation of the Bible.

It appears that the inner Collective of Christianity has a code language—Christianspeak. Listening to one Biblical literalist is just like listening to all of them. They have a standard set of zingers that they hear and repeat; they acquire learned responses to certain accusations or questions. Sometimes the code is merely a terse slogan, such as "God is good" or "Jesus saves." Other times, phrases are strung together, creating the semblance of a language that can go on for paragraph after paragraph. For example: "All humans are unregenerate in the Spirit and hate the thought of putting their hearts under the Will of the All-Loving God; only through His grace is the Truth made known to us, allowing our sinful natures to be cleansed in the Redeeming Blood of Our Lord Jesus Christ."

What you have, in actuality, is a language built around an idea without substance. God is invisible, unknowable, and yet he is assigned attributes that are in reality meaningless: omnipotence, omnipresence, omni-benevolence, Trinitarian. In order to make these attributes meaningful, they are themselves imbued with more nonsensical ideas: almighty, supreme, First Cause, love itself, Father, Son, Holy Spirit. From there, more vague words and ideas are added until Christians are speaking without actually saying anything. Their language is spattered with words and phrases like: glorification, justified, regeneration, righteousness, salvation, sanctification, tribulation, gifts of the spirit, let Jesus into your heart, be filled with the holy spirit, sins of the flesh, cleansed by the redemptive blood of Christ, etc.

Biblical Christians absorb this code language in church and from books and pass it on, sometimes adding their own slant or embellishment. If an outsider stops them and starts asking what exactly they mean by the things they say, they sometimes get thrown off...but only for a moment or two. Just like the Grinch inching his way out of a tough spot in the chimney, they maneuver around difficulties with more Christianspeak.

How Christians approach atheism

Over the years I've heard (and read) plenty of questions and comments from Christians. I understand that it's difficult to relate to atheism when you are well entrenched in god-belief; it's difficult for theists to be in my shoes. One of the problems I have seen with Christianity is that its adherents accept certain ideas about atheism proffered by the Collective that make them comfortable.

The following are the most frequent questions and comments I hear from Christians. Any atheist approached with these comments is likely to have heard them dozens of times already couched in very little variety of Christianspeak.

"How can you be an atheist?"

I really enjoy this one because it expresses the audacity they see in my merely lacking a belief that they themselves hold to be truthful. "How can you possibly not believe what I believe?" I was never indoctrinated into theism or supernaturalism. (Neither was I indoctrinated into atheism.) Once evidence of gods and a supernatural realm were presented to me, I found the propositions to be without merit. I don't see the outrageousness in that position.

"How did the universe get here?
How did the Earth get here?
How did we get here?"

What do these questions have to do with believing in gods? I don't understand why answers are so urgently required. Life is a mystery and there are scary things happening around us. I suppose it's comforting to believe you are protected and will live forever...but, what these questions imply is that if we don't have the answers, there must be a god. I don't see the connection.

"If there is no god, what is man's purpose?"

I, personally, don't believe that mankind has a purpose. But if he does, I don't know what it is and, frankly, no one else does, either. Why can't man have a purpose if there isn't a god? Isn't there any possible chance that aliens from another galaxy spawned life on Earth as a science experiment? That hypothesis seems just as likely to me as the idea of a god who created humans for the purpose of worshiping him.

"You are denying god."

I am of the opinion that the verb "deny" is an active word. I can't deny something that isn't there and I have no god-concept. To me, god isn't there. I can't deny something I don't believe exists. I don't accept the existence of gods because I haven't seen any evidence that they do exist; but I don't deny any existing gods. All an existing god needs to do is present itself to me and I'll willingly accept that it exists. After that, we can deal with its demands.

"You just don't want to live with the consequences of obeying God."

This is usually said with a flair for self-righteousness and it is a flagrant insult. I live a moral life on a par with the Christians I know. The only meaningful difference is that I don't worship a god. If that's the worst crime I ever commit, I at least commit it for good reason—I can't worship something that I don't believe is there. To pretend to worship when I don't believe would be dishonest.

"Pray to God for a sign."

I have been told to get into my dark closet and pray to God fervently and he will show himself to me. Not necessarily there in the closet and not as a physical presence, but I will receive some sign. What is to be taken as a sign from God? If I should feel a twinge, is that a sign? If I get a letter with money included a few days after my closet time, is that a sign? If I almost get in a car accident a week later, is that the sign? What of all the other times these things happened without the closet beseeching of the god? How do I tell the difference between coincidence and a sign? How can such mundane occurrences be signs of the existence of the almighty god of the universe?

I read an article in the newspaper recently about a woman who lost her trailer in a tornado. She prayed to God to save her roof. He saved the roof, but nothing else...except her life. She claimed that God answered her prayer. I just don't see it. I read in a *Dear Abby* column recently too, about some women who found a few pennies on the ground outside a car dealership and took it as a sign that their dear departed wanted them to buy a car at that place. It was really just a sign that someone dropped some pennies and didn't pick them up.

I won't give supernatural meaning to normal occurrences without good reason to do so. God is just too subtle for me; he's going to have to hit me hard over the head. I've heard he's not willing to do that, which only leads to my belief that I am closer to right on this one: there isn't a god there. People have been taught he's there, they are comfortable with him being there, they believe he's there; but that's not enough for me.

"You are atheist just because you choose to be."

I can't believe that anyone just wakes up one morning and decides to be an atheist. I think that Christians believe this because to them, atheism is a belief system and a belief is something you adopt. They *became* Christians actively by saying a prayer and dedicating their lives to Jesus. People tend to project their own views onto others and that is why Christians so often think that atheists choose to be nonbelievers; but it's not true. Atheism isn't something I decided to believe; it's the label I felt best described my lack of belief. Atheism isn't a club you join; it's just a word that describes nonbelief in deity.

I've read posts by believers doubting their faith on The Secular Web message boards. They say, "I'm thinking of becoming an atheist." You don't decide to *become* an atheist. You think about what you believe and if you decide you no longer believe it, maybe the atheist label describes your newfound position.

I don't choose to be atheist. It is just something that I am.

"Atheists say there is no god but to know that, you would have to know everything and you don't. So really, you're an agnostic."

If it makes Christians more comfortable to use agnostic instead of atheist, they can do so, but they would be wrong. If truth and honesty and correctness mean anything to them, perhaps they might rethink the whole thing.

Agnosticism is related to atheism. Atheism means without theism, without belief in deity. Agnostics believe that we can't know the truth of the proposition regarding the existence of deity; they usually have no belief in deity as well. Anyone who has no belief in deity is an atheist.

I am sure there are many atheists who say, "Gods do not exist." That is a plausible assertion considering the lack of evidence of gods in our world. I realize that to Christians, there is ample evidence but to the skeptic, it's all subjective emotionalism and hearsay. That's not evidence to a rationalist.

As to the idea that we need to know everything to know whether or not gods exist, that may be true but then we have to know everything to know whether or not gnomes, fairies, invisible pink unicorns and gabblecronks exist. Are Christians agnostic with regard to those entities? Or are they willing to say that they don't exist?

"Jesus was either Lord, liar or lunatic. He wasn't a liar or a lunatic, so he must have been God."

This is a beautiful example of the Collective and Christianspeak. They heard one guy say it (C.S. Lewis) and now they repeat it again and again as if it makes sense. They call it the "Trilemma," but it's really a false dilemma. The choices offered are all meant to lead to the preferred conclusion of Jesus as Lord. Lewis offers only three choices as if they are the only options available to us: He was a perfect god, a pathological liar, or a crazy person.

Christians are unable or unwilling to think outside the box, outside the Collective-approved quips. If they could, they'd see other possibilities: maybe Jesus was just a man with some good ideas, elevated to godhood by zealots; maybe he really believed what he was saying but was just mistaken; maybe he was talking about a different god; maybe the people who quoted him got it wrong; maybe he didn't exist and people made the stories up; maybe the theology is patterned after a pagan god. There are other options.

"If you believe in God and you turn out to be right, you haven't lost anything, but you've gained eternal life. If you don't believe and you are wrong, you've lost everything and will suffer an eternal torment."

The funny thing about Pascal's Wager is that whenever someone says it to me, they presume that I've never heard it before when I've heard it dozens of times, and they act as if it is a profound argument when it's anything but. Pascal's Wager can be approached several ways.

People don't choose to believe or disbelieve a proposition. I can't just start believing that gods and a supernatural realm exist. Try to make yourself believe something that you don't. Believe that the moon is made of green cheese. Believe that an Invisible Pink Unicorn is in your closet. You can't do it. You'll know that you are lying to yourself. I can't believe something that I don't, no matter how much evil Christians threaten me with.

Pretending that I believe in something that I don't, in my opinion, would be dishonest and therefore, I would lose a great deal—namely, my self-respect. I can't imagine anyone else would respect me if they knew I was pretending. Deeper than merely pretending, however, is the issue of believing in something because you've been taught to, told to, or because it's habit. I think that sort of belief is also dishonest; but I agree it is not a purposeful deceit...we can't help being human. Believing in something when there is no evidence of its validity is wrong, in my opinion. People who do so haven't thought much about what they believe; they aren't living consciously.

Another problem is the idea that a god would accept my belief and admiration simply out of respect for the odds or fear of punishment. Is that love? Is that a relationship? Is that justice? Is that what God wants from me?

Pascal's Wager can be used against Christians too. While some may agree that Allah is the same god as theirs, they don't believe the Koran is the word of their god, and yet, it is claimed that Mohammed is the latest prophet of the God of the Hebrews. If they don't believe in Mohammed, they've rejected Allah and they have lost everything. There could exist some other god than the Christian god; we don't know because we don't know everything. How can they know if they're worshiping the correct god in the proper way? Be careful, you may have chosen the wrong god to worship and for that, you may pay the ultimate penalty.

And finally, let's suppose that the god Pascal's Wager is designed to support does indeed exist. This god will make nonbelievers suffer simply because they could not believe. In my opinion, that is immoral. No one should be punished for what he believes or doesn't, and certainly not forever. I will not follow an immoral leader and I would not worship an immoral deity. Belief in the torture of your enemies is a slippery slope (no matter how much you may "pain" for them and their fate) that can lead to immorality.

"God loves you, whether you love him or not; he wants you to know him."

All God has to do is show himself to me. Convincing me of his existence isn't forcing me to love and worship him. I can still reject him—no free will problem there. But, let's face it; if someone I've never met wants a relationship with me, I'm going to have a problem if he never bothers to introduce himself. Christians say, "But he is trying to reach you through his word (the Bible) and through other Christians witnessing to you." Sorry, doesn't work. If someone wants a relationship with me and just sends me his autobiography and his friend to tell me about him, it's not going to do it for me, especially when his autobiography is filled with immorality, contradiction and error...although, he could still exist, he'd just not be as great as I was told he was.

The only answer I seem to get is that I have to really want him to come into my heart (like heart worms?) before he will. How can I want a deity that I don't believe exists to do something? I have to believe in him before he'll lead me to believe in him. However, if Christianity is true, it is the Christian god himself who decides whether or not I will believe. "So it depends not on a person's will or exertion, but upon God, who shows mercy...he has mercy upon whom he wills and he hardens whom he wills." (Romans 9:16-18) It has nothing to do with me, or Satan, or anything other than the will of God. If this god has willed that I should not believe, why do Christians find it necessary to vilify me? Aren't they, by doing so, saying that God's will is evil?

It's not as if I haven't already done the closet praying thing, so, I guess God is just too subtle for me...either that or he doesn't want me to believe in him...or he just doesn't exist and people are making it all up because they really want there to be more to life than...this.

"There are no atheists in foxholes."

That's not true, of course. I've communicated with atheists who did go to war and fought and watched others die. There have been plenty of atheists in foxholes. What this statement means to say broadly is that, when the chips are down, so to speak, when atheists are faced with death or harm or even a tough exam, they pray to a god. This is infuriatingly elitist and untrue. Atheists go through their lives just fine without having to appeal to a deity. Christians like to say things like that to make them feel sure of their beliefs. What it does, however, is evidence how insecure they actually are.

"Darwin and Madalyn Murray O'Hair now know that God exists."

This is another phrase that helps Christians feel secure. They have the truth and everyone will find out after they die that Christians were right all along. The way I see it, if you have to think things like this to make yourself secure in your beliefs, you ought to take a good hard look at yourself and see if there is anything there that needs to be right more than needs the truth; because you can't determine truth if your ego is in the way.

I heard the Christian groans in my head after that statement. They've told me I am the one with the ego problem. I reject God because of my egotistical view that I am in control of my own life. The difference is that I am first looking around me at the evidence of reality. Truth isn't about what I feel, want, think or imagine; it's about what is factual.

"Why don't atheists build hospitals?"

Atheists are often confronted with the lack of a concerted atheist front engaged in aiding the poor, oppressed and sickly. Look at all that Christians have done to help humanity, our accusers say. Where are the atheists in this struggle?

The answer is pretty clear; atheists are right there with the religious, feeding and clothing the poor, building homes for the homeless, and donating their time, goods and money to charities. That would be obvious to people, if they'd stop parroting what they've heard and think about what they're saying before repeating it to others. Why aren't there any hospitals built exclusively with atheist funds? Because atheists aren't herded into churches and preached to every Sunday; atheists aren't sheep. We're individuals who give to our communities individually.

But, the reason people attack atheists with this question doesn't really have anything to do with organizing atheists for charitable purposes. The real reason for the question is to attack the morality of atheists. The insinuation is that Christians build churches and go on missions because religion makes people moral and there are no atheist hospitals because atheists are immoral. That is simply untrue.

The Darwin fish being eaten by the Truth fish

Have you seen it? What this bumper sticker means is that an ethereal, elusive, ultimate Truth, based on subjective experience and revelation from a transcendent entity, and interpreted by your local preacher, trumps physical evidence. What Christians are saying to the world when they put this sticker on their cars is, "Don't confuse us with the facts."

"Why do you pick on Christianity?"

Christianity is the religion of my culture. It's all around me; it's on every street. It talks to me in the pithy sayings on church bulletin boards, some of which are quite rude. Most everyone I know believes in the reality of gods and demons, a man being crucified as a blood sacrifice (like that's a wonderful thing) then rising from the dead, and that one day the streets will run red with the blood of the wicked.

Because Christianity is the prevalent religion in my society, it is the religion I studied. I found that Christianity isn't what most Christians think it is, at least it's not what they keep telling me it is. I found it to be immoral and speaking out against immorality can't be bad. I found it to be a lie, and striving for truth is a good thing.

"Don't you like anything about Christianity?"

Yes, I do! I love the architecture of many churches, especially the older ones. I enjoy the music, especially at the winter solstice. Some beautiful works of art were inspired of religious passion. I appreciate that it was Christianity that brought Santa Claus and reindeer into my life (though I can't give it credit for the Easter bunny and egg hunts; the pagans have my gratitude for that). If belief in Christianity has turned some rotten people into good people who wouldn't otherwise have conformed, I'm glad.

I appreciate that Christianity evolves. While there will always be those persons who need to maintain a dogmatic, Biblical belief, Christianity also appeals to loving and tolerant people who can glean from it a positive and accepting religion.

Chapter Thirteen

How to Approach an Atheist

Christian (initiating the conversation): How did you become an atheist? Were there certain events in your life that propelled you in that direction? Or is it something you just woke up believing one morning?

Atheist: I'm not sure, but maybe you meant to ask why I'm an atheist, instead of how I became one. "How" implies I had a choice.

Christian: Ahh. You don't think you had a choice in the matter?

Atheist: No, I don't. I did figuratively "wake up" over a period of days; but not to "believing" something... atheism is a lack of belief.

Christian: I'm curious to know why you say that atheism is not a belief.

Atheist: A—without; theism—belief in deity. I am without belief in deity. Atheism is not a belief.

Christian: Certainly it is! Certainly, it is your faith. True?

Atheist: Why did you even ask? I said it wasn't a belief. You seem to be calling me a liar.

Christian: You seem to have a disdain for Christians. True?

It was all downhill from there. Though the conversation above is an abbreviated and paraphrased form of one I actually had, it is typical of my conversations with theists.

It's important for atheists and Christians to communicate, to share our feelings and thoughts. There is no reason why we can't accept each other and treat each other with respect. We can honor people without having to laud their beliefs; we only have to acknowledge that we don't agree. But all too often, the conversation ends without any real communication having taken place. Naturally, from my perspective, the problem is on the side of the theists who don't seem willing to hear what the atheist is saying. Perhaps I am wrong; nonetheless, I offer some tips to Christians in the hopes of bettering our chances of real communication. No matter the intention, to debate or to befriend, I hope that this information will offer Christians an insight into the difficulties they may face in such an endeavor.

Accept the atheist's definition of himself

This is very important. Think about what you call yourself. The term Christian doesn't mean the same thing for everyone. There are Christians who don't accept other professed Christians as such. Just as an atheist must learn what a Christian means by his label, the Christian should take the time to learn what the atheist means. The biggest problem I have encountered with Christians is their insistence that they know what I believe, and the reasons I don't believe in their god. I am always told that I don't believe because the thought of a god is abhorrent to me or I don't want to subject myself to a higher authority.

If you want to engage an atheist, first discover what he means by the label. You must be willing to accept his definition of atheism and his reasons for labeling himself so. If he says he doesn't believe because he sees no evidence for gods, you must take him at his word. Admittedly, this causes problems for the Christian who would like to convert such an atheist, but you can attempt to outline what you consider evidence for God and hope for some agreement from the atheist.

Understand atheism

Accept that atheism is not a religion—it has no dogma. There are no principles of atheism. Atheism is nothing more than lack of belief in deity. If you want to know what a particular atheist holds to be true, you have to ask him. You'll get into trouble if you assume you know what a person thinks, feels and believes just because he calls himself atheist. In order to have an honest, friendly, open discussion with another human being, you have to be able to accept him as he is, not as you have prejudged him or expect him to be.

Atheists are normal everyday people, just like Christians. Some of us are rude and obnoxious. Some of us are quiet and sweet. Some are well-read and intellectual. Some are couch potatoes. We are regular people. If you meet an offensive atheist, don't judge all atheists by him. How do you like it when non-Christians judge all Christians by Jerry Falwell or Jim Bakker? All atheists don't think like Madalyn Murray O'Hair. Atheists are very different from each other. The only thing we are sure to have in common is lack of belief in deity.

Forget Pascal's Wager

The first time I heard Pascal's Wager was from a teacher in a low-level logic class in community college. I remember thinking, "Hmmm, was that logical?" Atheists don't believe that gods exist; we believe they are fiction. Threatening us with God's wrath is meaningless to us, if not a little humorous. It's difficult to take someone seriously when they re-peat Pascal's Wager, no matter how cleverly they think they've disguised it. It shows an acute lack of understanding of atheism and the Wager itself.

Never tell the atheist he is going to Hell

Atheists know that according to Christian theology we are destined for eternal torment but we don't believe that Hell exists. Threatening us with the prospect is meaningless; it doesn't scare us anymore than the boogeyman does.

On the other hand, if you don't believe in the traditional concept of Hell, don't offer this idea to the atheist as if you are assuring him that, despite his atheism, God still loves him. Doing so is rather self-righteous. Your best bet is to stick with discussions of what Hell may or may not be. Any attempts on your part to declare a truth without any evidence will be seen as dishonest.

Don't try to prove the Bible is true by quoting it as your source

Atheists don't believe that gods exist; therefore, we don't believe that any gods have revealed themselves, certainly not in a book written by men. Quoting from the Bible to show the atheist that there is indeed a god and Jesus was his son will get you nowhere fast. Quoting the Bible to try to prove your moral stance is superior because it is derived from the highest authority in the universe will get you into trouble too, especially if you happen to have come across one of the many atheists intimately familiar with the book. You're likely to hear quoted scripture that reveals the ugliness and immorality of your god.

You can't prove the Bible is the word of a god by quoting the scripture in the Bible that says so. You can't use the book to prove the book is true. If you want to argue that the Bible is the word of a god, you'll have to find some outside evidence to support it.

If you are debating the historicity of Jesus, the Bible could be used as one source but you can't expect the atheist to accept the Bible as anything more than fiction until it has been shown to be true. Suppose I tried to convince you that Scarlett O'Hara was a real person. I could read parts of *Gone with the Wind* to try to prove it to you but that wouldn't be forceful would it? I would have to prove to you that *Gone with the Wind* was true; then you could accept it as evidence that Scarlett really lived.

Accept the atheist's reasons
for feeling what he feels

Our society vilifies certain segments and when that aspersion succeeds in damaging the emotional health of that segment, society lays the blame for it on the behavior of the group in question. A perfect example is homosexuality. A portion of our society despises homosexuality; they consider it immoral, vile, dirty and ugly. They want no part of it themselves (at least not consciously or publicly) and don't want homosexuals to be open about their lifestyles. Homosexuality, they say, is a shameful behavior and should be wiped out; if they can't abolish it, they can at least force homosexuals to keep their affairs in the closet where they (the presumably good and moral people) won't have to see them. Then these people have the audacity to claim that most homosexuals are depressed and hostile and dare to say it is the result of being homosexual. I'd be rather depressed too, and not a little angry, if an outspoken portion of society considered me to be abnormal, unacceptable, and even vile.

Not strangely enough, that is precisely what "good" Christian people do to atheists. I am happy to say that a large portion of society has become more accepting of homosexuality and they now decry violence and bigotry against gays and lesbians. As well, it is no longer considered honorable to be racist or misogynous. Unfortunately there is one prejudice that it is still quite acceptable to hold: that against atheists. It is still permissible to call your enemy an atheist, as if that is the worst thing a person could be. No one will contradict representatives or authorities who call atheists immoral and tell us all to leave the country if we don't like good 'ole God-fearing American values.

Atheism is labeled as the destroyer of our national greatness, the aberration that pollutes our good country, communist, Satanic, etc. All evils of the world can be put at atheism's door and no one will dispute it; no one will stand up for the rights of the atheist community except atheists themselves.

Atheists will deal with this societal ostracism in various ways. Many aren't bothered by it at all; they have a community of friends, realize that their understanding of the world isn't widely held, but aren't bothered by what other people think and say about them. Still, most people want to be accepted and liked; it's a normal human desire. Feeling that you are different is difficult enough without knowing that what makes you different is considered evil and abhorrent to many others.

Some people never admit they are atheist; it's the last thing they would ever do. I don't blame them. I think it must be a sad way to have to live, never being fully honest with other people, maybe not even yourself, but being empathetic, I can understand it and I would not look down on the atheist who can't or won't admit it to others, even to himself. Some admit what they are and remain unhappy with the reaction they receive. When you encounter an atheist who seems angry, try to feel what it must be like to be in a small and denigrated minority. It's a natural human reaction to be angry at one's situation when so many people hate you for it and make no qualms about expressing that hatred, when so many people tell lies about what you are and who you are and everybody else accepts those lies as if they are true. It's not an easy situation in which to be.

When an atheist expresses anger or sadness, even depression, you mustn't assume that it is atheism that causes those feelings. It may be the reaction of the Christian community the atheist lives in that causes those feelings. If people were more accepting, tolerant and loving of people who are different from them, the different people could be happier. Of course, that's never going to happen because when you have a dogma that must, without question, be believed, you have to vilify and demonize anyone who refuses to accept it. But because mainstream Christianity demonizes atheism, doesn't mean individual Christians must go along with it.

If Christians want to approach atheists, in hopes of learning more about them, friendship, or trying to convert them, they must understand the situation atheists are in. Too often the atheist is told his anger arises from his denial of God, from his anger at God, or from his unwillingness to submit to God. Christians won't score any points with that attitude.

On the other hand, many theists are surprised to find that the happy, well-adjusted family down the street, the mom active in the PTO, or the homeschooling family next door is atheist. That's not the atheism they are presented with in church and in books written by Christian apologists. Unfortunately, people you'd least expect to be atheist can turn out to be; that's a result of the prejudice of Christian society. More and more atheists and non-Christians need to speak out in this country if we hope to be accepted.

Be willing to take as much as you give

One of the biggest problems I've encountered and witnessed in the atheist/Christian dialogue is the Christian unwillingness to be wrong. I know that Christians believe they are correct; of course they do; people don't believe things that they know are wrong. And yet, the Christian expects the atheist to admit a possibility that he is wrong. Christian/atheist discussions are usually one-sided. The Christian takes the position of teacher and expects the atheist to be his student. The Christian tells the atheist what he must do to find God, but is unwilling to take the opposite course and apply it to himself. As well, the Christian often insists that the atheist concede that gods are possible but is rarely willing to agree that the absence of gods is also possible.

A Christian might tell an atheist he must pray to God for him to reveal himself. In order to do this, however, the atheist must first admit that a god possibly exists to which to pray. Then he must be fervent in his desire for this god to reveal his presence. The atheist must take a humble, supplicant attitude before the greatness of this god and beg him to reveal himself, to manifest his spirit in the heart of the atheist. I have heard atheists accept this challenge, but logically, they want the

Christian to take a part in it as well. If the god in question does not reveal himself, the atheist might propose, is the Christian willing to admit that he doesn't exist? No, the Christian says, because he claims for himself the correct position and will not admit that he could be wrong. Why should the atheist accept all the necessary criteria for the test and the consequences of the result while the Christian accepts nothing when the test fails?

If I ask a Christian to do the closet praying routine for Isis or Osiris, Odin or Shiva, he thinks my request is ludicrous. Why? Because the Christian does not accept that he could be wrong. It is the atheist who must accept fallibility and when the test doesn't work, the atheist is blamed. He didn't pray hard enough; he didn't really believe; he wasn't earnest. Never is the possibility that the god in question simply doesn't exist considered.

A Christian might also tell an atheist to live for a specific period of time as if he believed in God; pray to him, seek his guidance and wisdom, read and study the scripture for a period of, say, three months. The Christian assures the atheist that, if he truly lives this way, immerses himself in the idea of Christianity, he will experience the presence of God and will feel the great joy and love of being Christian—he will come to know and believe in God. But the Christian is never willing to apply the test to himself. He is not willing to live as if he doesn't believe for three months to experience that his life would be no different, or maybe better as a nonbeliever. Neither is he willing to accept that he is wrong if the atheist does as he is asked but returns to atheism at the end of the specified time.

These are unfair tests. They assume their conclusion: that the atheist is the one who is wrong and simply needs to perform a certain way, think or feel a certain way and he will see the rightness of the Christian position. The existence of God is debatable; he either does or does not exist. That all people don't agree that a god exists, and that God hides and must be sought out is evidence that he isn't real. It has certainly not yet been shown that he is. The Christian must be just as willing to accept he is wrong as the atheist.

Determine what proper evidence is

Christians might, early in the dialogue, determine what the atheist would accept as valid evidence for God or Jesus. They will find that most atheists don't accept the evidence that they have as evidence at all. If they did, they'd be Christians. They mustn't assume, then, that the atheist is only atheist because he hasn't seen the evidence. Try to imagine being an atheist in this Christian-dominated country. It is highly unlikely that a person who knows he's an atheist and is willing to be labeled as such has no knowledge of Christianity and the evidence claimed in favor of it.

Rationalists require that deity be researched in an objective manner. The fact that we can't answer a particular question is no reason to insert god as the answer. Miracles must be beyond mere stories and legends; they must be verifiable. Considering the power and superiority of the god in question, the things that pass as miracles today are nondescript. Is that the best a god can do? Prophecy must be accurate beyond the odds and must be specific, not vague and so symbolic as to be interpreted in many different ways.

Christians should be warned, however, that a request to know what it would take to convince an atheist that God exists or that Jesus was his son might produce an odd response from an atheist friend. Too often, atheists are approached with just such a question and when they give their answer, are attacked for it. The atheist is told that he is making demands on God for a sign, which is an affront to God. The atheist is told that he is presumptuous to claim God owes him any evidence at all. I have also heard atheists called to account for not humbling themselves before God, for daring to even ask that God make himself known to them, a lowly, wretched human! So you see, often the question of what evidence I might accept for God and Jesus is really just an excuse to berate me. If I don't seem happy to answer the question, that would be why.

Avoid pat stories

There have been many stories spread around the Internet that some Christians offer as evidence for God. What they show, in actuality, is the gullibility of the believer who passes them on.

In one story, an elementary school class is being lectured by a teacher who points out that you can see the trees and the birds, but you can't see God so he obviously doesn't exist. Then a little girl pipes up and claims that the teacher must not have a brain because no one can see it. What a laugh we all have at the atheist teacher's expense...being bested by a child. Unfortunately, none of the children suggest they cut the teacher's head open; then they would all be able to see her brain. Or, perhaps a CAT scan would serve. You see, we *can* see the teacher's brain. We have seen human brains, so we know they exist.

We can't see the wind, but we know it exists because we can witness and measure its effects in the world. We can't see air, but we can analyze its molecular structure and its effects on the animal and plant life forms that use it. We can measure gravitational pull. We experience the emotion of love. All these things we can not see can be experienced, studied and discussed objectively. God is invisible and is not experienced objectively.

Another fable we get is the story of the logic professor in which he argues with a Christian student and gets flustered because the Christian student maintains his position. The professor holds up his piece of chalk and declares that if there is a god let him stop the chalk from falling to the ground; then he drops it. The chalk, instead of falling to the floor, lands in the cuff of the professor's pants. Or the professor proclaims that if there is a god, he will stop the chalk from breaking when it hits the ground and the chalk drops, bounces off something and hits the floor without breaking. Then all the students follow the Christian out into the hallway where he witnesses to them while the professor is humiliated. What exactly is this story supposed to show us beyond the credulity of college students? We are supposed to believe that it was a god who caused the chalk to fall into the cuff instead onto the floor? We are supposed to believe it was a god that caused the chalk to bounce off something and land softly so it wouldn't break? Is that the best a god can do? Couldn't a god have suspended the chalk in mid air, levitated it to the chalk board and wrote with it, "I exist?" And the horrible characterization of the college professor belies a prejudice against the intellectual community that I find disheartening.

Christians should avoid stories such as these when dealing with their atheist friends. If they serve you and your Christian friends, keep them between yourselves.

Don't belittle education

Rationalists, at least (I can't speak for all atheists), hold education in high esteem. "Intellectual" is not a dirty word. Why is it iniquitous for so many believers? From this side it looks like Christians don't like it because in order to educate yourself, you may have to give up some, if not most, of your beliefs. The hierarchies in control of the Christian churches are well aware that the more educated a person is, the less likely he is to believe in a literal Christianity. The natural answer is to demonize intellectualism. If a Christian wants to open a dialogue with an atheist, the last thing he should do is claim revelation, interpreted from a very old book or by his local preacher, is more accurate than scientific research in explaining our natural world. If a person can't respect science and learning, he may not want to approach an atheist at all.

Don't attack subjects
you don't know much about

If Christians want to attack evolution, they'd better learn as much about it as they can. If they want to attack an atheist's logic or morality or philosophy, they'd better do their research. True, they're likely to come across some atheists who can't offer good responses to their attacks. The best they'll get in response is a quizzical look—the atheist is thinking that what he's hearing doesn't sound quite right, but he's not sure why. If the Christian keeps at it, the atheist is likely to go to the computer or library and start learning about the subject.

From experience, I know that most Creationists know very little about evolution. They've taken all their information from the Creationist propaganda machine which is a poor choice if you want to engage a rationalist on the subject. Don't get your information from the pulpit or a book or website built on the foundation of refuting the subject. Go to the books and sites that deal with the science or philosophy behind the subject as told by those who adhere to it. And don't rely on just one venue for information. Don't read one book and decide you've learned all you can learn about that subject.

When I wanted to learn about Christianity, did I read about it at an atheist site or in a book by an atheist? No. To learn about Christianity you have to read Christian books and talk to Christians. I understand that many Christians will claim that I have misrepresented their theology here; but what I have learned about Christianity has come directly from Christians—from their books, their websites, personal conversations and emails. I recognize that they are all very different; atheists are all very different also.

On the other hand, when I wanted to learn about the history of Christianity did I read Christian books? No. I read books by historians. When I wanted to learn about evolution, I read science books. To learn what Creationists believe I looked at Creationist books and websites. Don't let the opposition tell you the facts about a subject. Go to the best educated people in that subject for your information. You don't have to believe what they say, but you'll at least be getting closer to the facts and less propaganda. Then go to the opposition for a response and see how they fare.

The problem with people who have a dogma to which they adhere is that they tend to look at others in the same light. If they have a truth that must be defended, they assume that people who study and talk about evolution must also have a truth to stand by. Dogmatic people are suspicious of science. That is a real problem and I don't know how to help with it except to say that you needn't accept everything the opposition says as truth, but, if you want to discuss the matter intelligently with its proponents, you must at least be versed in the subject from their viewpoint.

To put it bluntly, if you try to offer Creationist rhetoric to an intelligent atheist, he may laugh at you. I have yet to see anything offered by a Creationist that wasn't pure baloney. There are intelligent skeptics of evolutionary theories; but they are hardly Creationists.

Never say we evolved from monkeys

The first time I heard a Christian deride the theory of evolution by saying he "didn't come from no monkey" I thought it was a fluke. What's one person with a misunderstanding of speciation, after all? We can't all be scientists. But again and again I hear the same refrain from theists: evolution means we evolved from apes or monkeys. Worse, I get the question, "If we evolved from apes, why are there still apes? Why don't we see the apes changing into humans?" I have, more than once, stood at my door teaching a basic lesson on the origin of the human species to Jehovah's Witnesses and I'm not exactly a scientist. How is it that a non-scientist can understand these theories better than many Christians? Dogma—I don't have one.

Let me explain briefly here that humans did not evolve from monkeys or apes. Monkeys, apes and humans are all primates; we share a common ape-like ancestor. Monkeys evolved into monkeys. Apes evolved into apes. And humans evolved into humans. I can't believe the standards of science education in this country are so poor that I should have to explain that.

Mind Your Truth

"You can't understand the Bible until you are filled with the holy spirit."

"You don't understand the Truth because you are blinded by Satan."

"Worldly knowledge is foolishness to true Christians."

These things might be true, if what Christians believe is true. What they appear to be, however, is excuses, reasons Christians, from the inception of the religion, offer to explain why others question their beliefs. If the sciences seem to refute Biblical teaching, it's because science is "of the world" or scientists are blinded and biased. Only spiritual truth is real truth, all else is meaningless. The reason everyone is not Christian is because Satan blinds men to the truth, or because they are willful and disobedient. These are handy justifications to keep Christians from looking objectively at their beliefs. All you have to do is believe that you have the truth, the one and only truth, and the reason other people don't accept it has nothing to do with your beliefs. The problem is not your dogma, it's the nonbelievers themselves. That is a very convenient excuse to carry around. If someone is going to approach an atheist with these ideas in mind, I have to wonder why they would bother.

Chapter Fourteen

The Way I See It

What is tolerance?—it is the consequence of humanity. We are all formed of frailty and error; let us pardon reciprocally each other's folly—that is the first law of nature.

—Voltaire

All religion, every bit of it, is had through hearsay. Everyone is talking about the god who is there, but where? No one knows what it is, where it is, how it is or why it is, but they talk about it just the same, as if they know. No one ever experiences god personally. We listen to other people talk about it and read books; other people tell us what to believe, they interpret our subjective feelings as "god," but we can never know for sure because god is hidden.

Nonbelievers are expected to accept hearsay as valid evidence for god. That is how god wants us to know about him. He won't come directly to us; he sends his believers as mouthpieces, and his holy book as instructions. When we question believers, we realize that they know nothing beyond what they've been told by someone else or read in a book written by men. Occasionally someone comes on the scene saying something new and even traditional Christians admit those people are making it all up. Jim Jones wasn't a Christian, they say. Neither was David Koresh. They were false prophets. Listen to us, they say, we are the true prophets. Shadow play, hearsay, illusion, hope, self-righteousness and power—that is religion.

I don't believe that there was a conspiracy to take a Jewish carpenter and turn him into a god for the purpose of blinding the masses to gain power and wealth. I don't believe anyone purposefully deceived anyone else in the conception of the theology. I believe people were misguided by a misunderstanding of mythology and some cunning, unscrupulous people took advantage of the situation. It's not Christianity's fault; it was a natural mistake and a product of our culture that we would rally around a figure of salvation such as the Christ/Messiah. That's where we were in our history and clearly, many are not ready to move beyond it as yet.

I think Christianity is a lie because I don't believe that Jesus ever existed. I believe he was a mythical product of pagan Judaism, a pagan god, linked to the would-be historical figure of the Messiah. It is understandable that some thought he was a real man but, to me, it's a lie. All that is needed for me to change my mind is evidence to the contrary.

Another reason I can't accept Christianity as truth is because I don't believe that humanity is a vessel of sin that must be redeemed to be in the presence of a god. If a creator god exists, if we are God's children, we can't be so disgusting to him that we require a savior. What sort of perfect, loving entity creates loathsome beings?

I think of Christianity as the epitome of the parent/child relationship—an extension of it in adulthood—an escalation of it into something sacred and holy. The parent/child relationship at its best exemplifies unconditional love and acceptance. I would never punish my child for being human and certainly not forever. "But you are not God," is the response I've heard. To which I reply, that's correct; God would be unfathomably more accepting and loving than I, as a human mother, could be. How could I, as the created, be more beneficent toward my child than the omni-benevolent creator himself? If we allow our god to be anything less than we are we debase the concept so that it becomes the ultimate expression, not of the greatest, but of the vilest of man; we make it ugly.

Christianity gives people what they need. I can understand the anxiety that scientific advances bring to our society. The more we progress technologically, the more fearful we become; the more we learn about the vastness of the universe, the smaller and more insignificant we feel and the more we begin to think that everything we do is for naught. Salvation religions play on that fear. They say, yes, you are an insignificant, worthless creature...but you belong to a powerful father/god, thereby offering you hope that you have meaning and purpose, that you are significant, that your life will not end.

I can understand all of that. Part of me thinks it is alright to let people indulge their yearning; don't take away their solace; they need it. Another part of me thinks that a lie, no matter how comforting, can only be harmful in the long run. I do believe that the lie of salvation religions has been very harmful to our world.

Christians often point out to me the good that Christianity has brought about. They are either not well versed in history or choose not to consider the horrors that Christianity and other salvation religions have caused. Think how much more good might have come if we'd learned earlier that this life is the only life there is and that there is no other world, no Heaven. Long ago we may have stopped warring; we may have started helping our planet instead of abusing it; we may have actually seen the true worth in our fellow humans and learned what love really is. We can never do those things on a global scale until we stop looking to the hereafter for consolation and into the ancient past for values.

I don't like Christianity for several reasons. As good as the religion is for good people, it is even better for bad people. People use Christianity to promote hate and intolerance; they use the Bible to support their efforts to treat others despicably. Christians tell me this isn't the fault of their religion; it is the fault of sinful mankind. I don't see it that way. I think of god, if it exists, as a great and wonderful force. Christians tell me God is all-loving and this all-loving, omnipotent being gave us his word. How could the word of such a remarkable being have anything bad in it at all? How could it possibly be misused if it was all good?

The supposed word of God, the Bible, is not all good. It is filled with acts of murder, torture, rape, incest, deceit, hatred, war, vengeance, and lust. It is not the book of a loving deity; it's the book of tribal men. If a god existed that loved us and wanted us to live with him in a paradise, he would produce, even through inept men because he's so powerful, a book that was clear and unambiguously good. It would have nothing in it that could be misconstrued. That's why I will never believe that the Bible is the work of a god. My idea of god is different from most Christians'. My idea of god doesn't reflect man's idea of himself, it transcends it.

Some people have been shocked to hear me claim their religion is immoral. Others simply disagree; they have a different idea of morality than I do. What is immoral about Christianity? The biggest immorality is Hell. There is, by my moral standard, no justification for eternal punishment. Christians have wrestled with the concept of Hell for centuries and they've altered their interpretation to suit the changing morals of our society.

While some Christians continue to maintain that Hell is a tortuous and eternal punishment for sinners of all kinds, others have made different claims. Hell, some say, may not be eternal; the punishment will fit the sin or crime—but that is not a Biblical perspective. Many people are uncomfortable with the Biblical view; they take from it pictures of Christ and God that are palatable to them and claim that the parts they don't agree with or find discomforting are symbolic or tribal history, not the message of God.

Christianity is inexorably linked to the Bible. If you're not going to take the whole thing, why take only parts you like? If you've decided that Hell is anything other than eternal torment, you've recreated Christianity to suit your sensibilities. If you can do that, how is it that you can claim that any part of the Bible is the true word of your god? As long as Christianity is part of the Bible, it will be immoral. Maybe one day, a thousand or so years from now, there will be a new Christianity, totally separate from the tribal war god, Yahweh. That will just be more evidence that man makes religion, not gods.

Christianity furthers elitism and intolerance. Many conservative Christians try their best to adhere to the entire Bible and that, while noble, is what will forever leave them with an immoral social outlook. The Bible offers ample justification for intolerance and hatred of other religions, other sects of Christianity, nonbelievers, homosexuals, and women. As long as the Bible is looked on as the word of their god, Christians will have to defend iniquity and injustice.

Luckily, most Christians don't read and study the Bible as if it were the absolute, pure, inerrant word of their god. They read it as an ancient history with many (questionable) morality tales and lessons. Anything that they don't agree with, or find immoral, they simply dismiss. Christianity is, in fact, evolving and changing.

Christians are no more immoral than anyone else. There are moral, upstanding Christians, just as there are moral upstanding Jews, Muslims, pagans, Wiccans, and atheists. The problem with Christianity is that immoral people can use its holy book for their own pernicious means.

Christians aren't immoral simply because they worship the god of the Bible. They've molded him to fit their own morality. They've adapted him. While certainly there are corrupt Christians who claim that they are perfectly just in their misanthropic behavior because it is God-ordained, is it possible for a good, moral person to become immoral by adhering to a literal interpretation of the Bible? I believe so.

It begins with Hell and elitism. The normally good person accepts that some people are less deserving of Heaven than they themselves. Worse, people who merely don't believe the way they do are deserving of eternal torture by the god they call loving. These good people begin to equate love with torture, with Hell, with evil. They allow themselves to become bigoted against certain others in society. They don't call themselves bigots (what bigot does?); they call themselves the righteous, the good. What does that do to a person's idea of morality? Punishment is love; torture is justice; bigotry is goodness. It's a short, slippery slope from that point to hatred and intolerance of all but those they agree with in every aspect of life.

Many Christians openly oppose tolerance. Tolerance to them means acceptance of sin and evil. But tolerance is appreciating our differences, allowing that we are not the only standard bearers, and realizing that we can not make all the rules for all the people. Tolerant people understand that no human has the only truth about deity. No one knows for sure if there is one. Those who believe that the Bible is the word of the one and only god only *believe* it. They don't *know* it to be true because there is no god here and now substantiating their claim. They must *believe* it because there is no evidence to support their position. Someone else could be right. The Muslims could be right. The Hindus, the pagans, the atheists could be right. Theists can't know for sure.

Intolerance is adamantly proclaiming that your way is the right way and everyone else is wrong—your interpretation of the word of your god in your holy book is the only right way. That's intolerance, elitism and bigotry. It's very unattractive and seamy but there will always be a segment of society that requires the feeling not only of being right, but of being one of a select few who are. It's an immoral view, an immoral attitude and an immoral way to live. I want no part of it.

Since realizing I was atheist, I have faced many theists, most Christian, who have mislabeled me, misunderstood me and despised me. It seems from this side that Christians can't stand to look at the possibility that they are mistaken and they have to make atheists into something we are not to make themselves feel more secure. They hate us for pointing out to them, by our mere existence, that they could be wrong.

I am often reminded of the story of the *Emperor's New Clothes* by Hans Christian Anderson. If you recall, the emperor commissioned two scoundrels to make him a set of new clothes from the finest fabric in the world, invisible to ignorant and stupid people. When the emperor found he couldn't see the cloth, he knew he had to keep his ignorance secret. He then paraded his new outfit in front of the populace, confident that only stupid people would think he was naked. All the people admired his clothes so no one would think they were dumb. But a small boy, as children are more honest and forthright, stood in front of the throng and declared, "The emperor is naked!" The boy was scolded; but gradually everyone began to agree that the emperor was, indeed, naked. The emperor, too embarrassed to admit the truth (that he'd been had), continued on his merry, naked way.

Atheists are like the honest boy who didn't understand why everyone was claiming clothes when no clothes could be seen. The adults didn't appreciate his honesty because it forced them to question their willingness to believe. Atheists don't want to pretend we see things that aren't there just to keep believers from feeling threatened.

I can't help that I don't believe what Christians believe; I can't help that I've come to think of their religion as a lie. I think they are wrong, just as they think I am. They believe their position is correct as strongly as I believe mine is. Our only options are hatred and intolerance or love and acceptance.

I don't think Christians are stupid, as I have been accused by some. I think they are credulous—willing to believe more easily than I am. I am more skeptical. I don't know why; I just am. That doesn't mean there is something wrong with me or that I am bad. It doesn't mean that I am better than believers, or that they are superior to me. We're just different. We should, both sides, be able to accept that simple fact: we are different.

I imagine that many people will claim I have misidentified Christians and maligned Christianity. I've pointed to a small subset of Christians, they may say, and attacked their brand of the theology, instead of seeing Christianity as it really is: liberal, loving, and tolerant. I hope that is true. I hope there is a huge majority of Christianity that doesn't adhere to the doctrines of Hell and Biblical literalism. If they are out there, where are they?

According to recent statistics, there are some thirty million Americans who do not subscribe to any religious identification; where are they? Hidden? They are quiet, independently living their lives without stirring up trouble, marching on Washington, or typing out scathing replies to others on the editorial pages. I feel it's time they stood up and were counted—it's time to let the world know we are here in all our varieties, under all our labels (or without label), and we won't allow a theocracy in this country.

Perhaps the same independence and complacency infects the majority of liberal Christians who I am told are "out there," because the Christianity I am confronted with regularly, via the bookshelf, television, and Internet is evangelical, radical, and pro-theocracy. If liberal Christianity is the norm, it needs to stand up and denounce the aggressive "religious right" that would lead this country away from its base of freedom for all people.

This is the way I see the religious: the principles they accept of their theology reflect their true personalities. Intolerant elitists become hateful extremists, taking all the worst parts from an ancient book to further their selfish aims. Kind, loving moderates take from the religion of their culture gentle, peaceful teachings, and practice acceptance.

Which sort of believer are you?

A Bibliography

I wouldn't want anyone to read my thoughts and opinions and take them as fact, based simply on their presence in a published book. Naturally I would encourage people to find their own answers through reading and research. Following is a list of just a few of the books and websites that were helpful to me in my search for truth. For a more comprehensive listing of my library, including the apologetics titles I've read, visit the Reading Room at *www.atheistview.com*

Armstrong, Karen. *A History of God*. Knopf, 1993.

Barker, Dan. *Losing Faith in Faith: From Preacher to Atheist*. FFRF, Inc., 1992.

Berra, Tim. *Evolution and the Myth of Creationism*. Stanford Univeristy Press, 1990.

Drange, Theodore M. *Nonbelief and Evil: Two Arguments for the Nonexistence of God*. Prometheus Books, 1998.

Finkelstein, Israel and Silberman, Neil Asher. *The Bible Unearthed: Archaeology's New Vision of Ancient Israel and the Origin of its Sacred Texts*. Free Press, 2001.

Freke, Timothy and Gandy, Peter. *The Jesus Mysteries: Was the "Original Jesus" a Pagan God?* Harmony Books, 1999.

Fromm, Erich. *The Dogma of Christ and Other Essays on Religion, Psychology, and Culture*. Henry Holt, 1955.

McKinsey, C. Dennis. *The Encyclopedia of Biblical Errancy*. Prometheus Books, 1995.

Moreland, J.P. and Nielsen, Kai. *Does God Exist? The Debate between Theists and Atheists*. Prometheus Books, 1993.

Russell, Bertrand. Seckel, Al; editor. *Bertrand Russell on God and Religion*. Prometheus Books, 1986.

The Secular Web library at www.infidels.org

Shermer, Michael. *Why People Believe Weird Things: Pseudoscience, Superstition, and Other Confusions of Our Time*. Freeman, 1997.

Wheless, Joseph. *Forgery in Christianity* and *Is it God's Word?* Kessinger Publishing Company.